3670

HO
E W
JEHOVAH'S
WITNESSES

D0642010

HOW TO E WITNESS TO JEHOVAH'S WITNESSES

WILLIAM J. SCHNELL

BAKER BOOK HOUSE
Grand Rapids, Michigan

A NOTE FROM THE AUTHOR

I have received a request to show proof that I was with the Watch Tower Society. Apparently, throughout the world, wherever my character is not attacked it is being suggested that I was never with the Watch Tower.

I realize that this poses difficulties, as many Jehovah's Witnesses are being told that I do not exist on their lists.

I am hereby submitting my ordination paper, which I swear is a true facsimile of the original.

CERTIFICATE

THIS IS TO CERTIFY THAT

<u>W. J. SCHNELL</u>

has declared himself as a follower of Jesus Christ and wholly consecrated to do the will of Almighty God;

That he has taken a course of study of the Bible and Bible helps prescribed by this Society and that he has shown himself apt to teach and to preach "this gospel of God's Kingdom" under Christ Jesus (Matthew 24:14); and that he has the Scriptural ordination to preach this gospel of the Kingdom.—Isaiah 61:1, 2; Isaiah 52:7

Therefore he is hereby declared by this Society as a duly ordained minister of the gospel and is authorized to represent this Society and to 'preach this gospel of the kingdom', proclaiming the name of Jehovah God and Christ Jesus as King.

Dated <u>October 31,</u> 19 37

WATCH TOWER BIBLE & TRACT SOCIETY

By _U. A. If___

Vice-President

From the office of the
Watch Tower Bible and Tract Society
Brooklyn, New York

FOREWORD

THE Lord graciously took me by the hand in the Fall of 1956 and made me appear in the midst of CHRISTIANITY in the precincts of 48 different denominations. Here, across the United States and Canada, I came to know Christianity in a way as perhaps no other man knows today.

Why do I say this? I came into the midst of Christianity as a rebel from the Jehovah's Witness heresy, still filled with the doctrines of heresy, which I knew well. The Lord caused my association with Christianity to debunk these heretical doctrines promulgated by reason, and gradually, by faith, brought the true doctrines of Christianity into my consciousness. In this manner the long night of reasonings ended in revelation.

But soon, speaking in chapel periods in seminaries, Bible schools, colleges, ministeriums, churches, Sunday schools, seminars, I became aware of a very serious defect in Christian thinking. With consternation I came to the full realization that Christianity was asleep.

No wonder Jehovah's Witnesses and others like them rode rough-shod over the clergy, defeated the Christians at their own doors, made them afraid of them. I was now shocked. What was wrong?

While in the cults 100 per cent participation of all was demanded and achieved, I observed in Christianity only a small handful of pastors and laymen carry the whole load of witnessing for Christ. Most Christians, who today call themselves laymen, do not even know how to give an account "of the faith that is within them", much less can they "EARNESTLY CONTEND FOR THE FAITH ONCE DELIVERED TO THE SAINTS".

There is something deadly wrong here. When the Lord Jesus appeared, He called disciples. From Mark 1: 16–20 we observe how He did that. He did not call idle men but such who were faithfully performing their duties. The call was first an invitation, "Come ye after Me". Here they were invited to come to Him to enrol in training school. The curriculum was living with Jesus, following Him observing His work,

7

receiving private instructions, and finally being sent out to practise what they had learned. These first twelve were called "apostles", which in English means "sent ones". Soon thereafter the Lord Jesus trained an additional seventy and sent those out too, and thus personal evangelism began. Observe, the call also included a promise, "I will make you to become fishers of men."

Here, in a nutshell, the purpose of the call of Jesus is stated. In one way or another every follower of Christ is to have a part in accomplishing His mission, the saving of the lost. Christian, the pastor is not the only one who is a fisherman in your congregation, with all of you as inactive laymen sitting in the pews and looking on. Fishing for men is the responsibility of all Christians. Not all are called to be pastors, preachers, teachers, but by life (as soul winners); prayer (lighters of the Lord's candle which is the spirit of man); Testimony (which is witnessing for Christ); in every way the Holy Spirit directs; each follower of Christ has been called to become a fisher of men. If qualifications are lacking, remember Jesus said: "I will *make* you."

In the Watch Tower movement I was for years a *Zoneservant*. As such I trained thousands of Jehovah's Witnesses in the arts of WITNESSING, EVANGELIZING AND SOULWINNING.

Now that the Lord has saved me, and liberated my mind from heresy, He called me into your midst, gave me the finest platform a man ever had and provided me with opportunity for an intimacy which few today command regarding present Christian thinking. In all, I am completely free of sectarian and denominational views.

In this manner, you see before you an analysis of your condition before the Lord. Read the seven chapters of this book very carefully. Then make up your mind whether you are called by the Lord Jesus. If you are, then make it count. Eight lessons in the book will show you how to do it. Remember Jesus said, "I will make you." Let the Lord train you, send you, become a fisher of lost souls.

CHRISTIANS: AWAKE! is a last call! The cults, as well as atheism and agnosticism, are closing in. Will the sleeping giant, CHRISTIANITY, awaken in time? I believe he will. May this book help in this direction.

W. J. S.

CONTENTS

		Page
Foreword	. . . . .	7

Chapter

I.	How to Witness to Jehovah's Witnesses	.	11
II.	How to Use Truth Versus Error	. .	33
III.	How to Witness for Christ (Acts 1:8)	.	56
IV.	How to Evangelize for Christ or Make the Personal Contact (Prov. 27:17)	. .	76
V.	How to Win Souls for Christ (Prov. 11:30)	.	99
VI.	How to Organize the Training, Teaching and Telling Plan (Acts 2:41–47)	. . .	116
VII.	How to Organize Group Witnessing	. .	141

HOW TO WITNESS TO JEHOVAH'S WITNESSES

COMBATING OF THE SO-CALLED "GOSPEL OF THE KINGDOM" PREACHED BY THE JEHOVAH'S WITNESSES

THE gospel of the kingdom preached by the Jehovah's Witnesses with such zeal, consummate skill and unusual persistency, is generated from out of the offices of the Watch Tower Bible and Tract Society, Inc., 124 Columbia Hts., Brooklyn 2, N.Y., U.S.A.

For this reason it fans out from an earthly centre. Its drawing power must of necessity be a horizontal one. Unlike the knowledge of our Lord Jesus Christ, which we ardently hope will "cover the earth as the waters cover the sea" (Hab. 2: 14), it has created for itself a stream, or, as they themselves put it, a "channel", upon which to traffic in order to draw.

Other streams have been etched out in this manner in times past. There are, for instance, two great philosophical systems or streams (which shall be minutely discussed in other chapters) known as "Otherworldliness" and "Thisworldliness". In this same sense the NEW WORLD SOCIETY of Jehovah's Witnesses has become a stream best described as "Outerworldliness" (which will be discussed in my coming large book, *Is The New World Society of Jehovah's Witnesses Christian?*). It is a brand-new philosophy. It shares in common with other cults the distinction of *not* being a religion or a theology. It is a philosophy.

These three synthesizations of the past two millennia are human adaptations, designed to blunt the power of the gospel of Jesus Christ.

Because of its "Outerworldly" character, the Watch Tower Society has succeeded in perfecting "this gospel of the kingdom" to be preached by Jehovah's Witnesses, fashioning it to become the drawing power, or the current, of its stream. This drawing power is horizontal. To date it already has drawn into its current 1,100,000 persons as baptized Kingdom Publishers, and some 10,000,000 persons have been induced to enter it. These you find involved in various stages. Some up to their ankles, barely getting their feet wet. Others already up to their knees. Still others up to their thighs. And a few already up to their necks. The last-mentioned are close to becoming Kingdom Publishers, who either have to swim or sink in the theocratic works-righteousness tide of the stream in order to live in it. Continuing to use this picture, we observe in all the traffickers of this stream that everyone who swims in it must go out and engage, witness to and train new ones to become swimmers or Kingdom Publishers in this NEW WORLD SOCIETY. Herein lies this system's challenge to Christianity!

GENERATING HORIZONTAL POWER TO DRAW

The gospel of Jesus Christ has vertical drawing power (John 6: 44; John 12: 32), wherein the Holy Spirit regenerates and upholds. The gospel of the kingdom preached by the Jehovah's Witnesses has many limitations. To produce maximum pressure, it fell prey to a most glaring one, which is its time limitation between 1914 and Armageddon on the one hand, and space compression of separation into a narrow stream or channel of exclusivism on the other hand. Because it draws horizontally, the Watch Tower Society has had to devise a swift pace, current and tempo in order to create maximum suction-like drawing power. These inbuilt pressures of limited time and limited space are its cardinal weaknesses and will be its undoing.

At first, under Russell's tenure, the method and orbit devised was simple enough. The Watch Tower Society began to declare "the approach of the end of the world." That meant in their thinking, and from Scripture this appeared quite plausible in this context, that the harvest of the age was beginning. The gospel Russell fashioned, therefore, in the main, became the HARVEST GOSPEL.

The newly created Watch Tower Society (1884) in this scheme became the new bin into which the separated wheat was drawn out of all Christendom. Horizontal drawing power was quite cleverly devised by him. He used publicized sensationalism. His slogan "The Lord returned invisible to human eyes in His Second Coming in 1874" was truly sensational. It served to draw many into this new bin, who, in being accepted as wheat by Russell, were flattered to think of themselves as the "holy people."

However, in order to keep matters in motion he invented sustaining drafts. These were something similar to "channel locks" which lift water to higher levels in a channel. Between 1884 and 1914 he offered, in addition to these, prophetic winds to sail with, in such predictions as: (1) that the world will come to an end in 1914; (2) that Armageddon would be fought in 1914; (3) that the gathered-in saints, or the "holy people" Russellites, would be taken to heaven.

The subsequent shock of non-fulfilment of these expectations of 1914, coupled with the disaster of Russell's death in 1916, almost stilled the current of drawing power. The heavenly aspect of his expectations, so brazenly misused, certainly were forever untenable in Watch Tower circles.

A Gospel on a Lower Plane had to be Fashioned.

The newly elected leaders of the Watch Tower Society, who were ushered into office early in 1917, had to organize new and different facets for drawing power. This task they accomplished within fourteen years between 1917 and 1931. (Later I will enumerate the 148 changes made during this time, with actual proof from Watch Tower literature.)

Matthew 24, a great prophecy, became to them by interpretation THE POWER. Through adaptation of it to their policy they ventriloquized their new version of the end of the world by saying that Matthew 24 began to be fulfilled with 1914, when World War I started.

To give this new gospel the same type of historical connotation as Russell had given his so-called HARVEST GOSPEL, they called it "this gospel of the kingdom" preached for a witness until the end would come (Matt. 24: 14). With this switch they had first to play down, then eventually forget about, the hope projected by the gospel of Jesus Christ, namely, to find a future home in heaven (1 Pet. 1: 3–4).

The makings of this situation forced them subsequently to forget the gospel of promise and, like others before them, turn their faces upon works and law. A "mess of potage" was concocted (148 changes) to feed the tremendous appetite for achievement and works raised by this new gospel of works, as it jelled within the pressurized exclusivism of the NEW WORLD SOCIETY and became compressed into the limited time between 1914 and Armageddon. This "mess of pottage" became the food for Jehovah's Witnesses in "due season" so that they would not feed on the Word of God and upon Christ the bread from heaven. It was continually prepared in the columns of the *Watch Tower* between 1917 and 1931. In its treatment of Scripture the *Watch Tower* raised a fleshly vista for a NEW WORLD SOCIETY apposite of "an undefiled inheritance in heaven" promised by our Lord Jesus Christ (John 14: 2; 1 Pet. 1: 3). Devious arguments to uphold *Watch Tower* heresies by misusing the Bible were thus invented, and now the Watch Tower Society has incorporated all of these errors into its NEW WORLD TRANSLATION of the Scriptures, where the Scriptures "have been wrestled with to their own destruction." (My book *Thirty Years a Watch Tower Slave* furnishes you with an authentic eye-witness account of these developments.)

By misuse of Matthew 24: 14, the gospel of Jesus Christ became "this gospel of the kingdom shall be preached in all the world for a witness . . . and then shall the end come." A narrow, limited time from 1914 to Armageddon was pinpointed as the only time in which to find salvation, projecting the hope that such faithful ones would be saved when this battle would be fought and won. Thus these were made to lose sight of this great truth that our salvation has not only been fought for but was won on the cross more than 1,900 years ago. This limited time element, and the narrow selection techniques to attain salvation by work, directed from the theocratic launching pad in Brooklyn, N.Y., U.S.A., form the dynamics which project the Jehovah's Witnesses into the world with apostolic zeal amidst NEW WORLD SOCIETY propaganda latched onto human uncertainties and troubles. This *modus operandi* is very much like the "material gains nuclear threat employed by the THISworldly communistic system," also a society of the flesh, and is without spirit and soul.

Here are some of the horizontal power facets developed by the NEW WORLD SOCIETY of Jehovah's Witnesses.

USE OF BACKDROP OF URGENCY

The historical basis for this pitch is the fact that World War I did begin in 1914. Another series of facts followed in its train, namely, a prolonged period of unsettlement and readjustment as the industrial revolution came of age. With these phenomena a whole generation of men became insecure overnight, and that in a hundred different ways. This worldwide insecurity is therefore now for us in the flesh a fact of life.

Originality, you see, was still the trait of the Watch Tower Society. They are clever in the use of propaganda. Dramatically they applied the prophecy of Matthew 24 to this period of history now current and which began in 1914. In this clever psychological manner the Watch Tower Society created for itself a high rampart, from which exalted position it could talk like an oracle of doom. It turned our Saviour God, who sits on His throne of grace, into a "wrathful Jehovah," and glibly predicted His coming off His throne of grace in 1914 and of setting up a position in the Temple in 1916 to begin judgments. This all, while the silence of God to this hour still attests our Lord's sitting upon His throne of grace. It subsequently published in its new books hammer-like judgments—first against the Russellites; then against all churches of Christendom; then against politics and commerce; engulfing everybody and everything, with only one exclusion: the NEW WORLD SOCIETY of Jehovah's Witnesses. This combination began to draw tens of thousands into the NEW WORLD SOCIETY. This conjuring up of time-and-end application of Matthew 24 from 1914 to Armageddon has been successfully used in feeding upon the insecurity now experienced by all mankind. Fleshly security wrapped in ideological slogans, which could be gained only by accepting and then preaching "this gospel of the kingdom," became the incentive.

USE OF TOTAL ATTACK

1926 saw another device perfected, commencing with the appearance of the book *Deliverance*, published by the Watch Tower Society. Here, as well as in all subsequent books published by the Society, we see voiced a concerted attack, declaring all religious, political and commercial organizations as being of the devil. All such are threatened in these books with total destruction in Armageddon.

This is graphically demonstrated for you, with much proof taken from these very books in the chapter "Who is the Big Bad Wolf?" in my book *Thirty Years a Watch Tower Slave*. Note how vociferous and insistent this attack became as time wore on. It was designed, believe it or not, to draw new converts into the NEW WORLD SOCIETY.

You ask: How can that be? How can you win people by attacking them?

Consider this. All large organizations attacked by the Watch Tower literature also have large minorities—minorities who often disagree with the majorities. In fact, many such have a grouse against the leadership. Often this shows in opposition and criticism. By attacking *all*, the NEW WORLD SOCIETY adroitly exploits these differences and grievances by drawing attention to itself as a "clean organization" able to champion them. Moreover, many such are drawn into this stream because of a kindred intensity of behaviour. Their own violent behaviour as opposition to the leadership in their own organizations attracts them to the violent and virulent attacks of the Watch Tower against their organizations. Thus such vociferous ones are drawn to this group, and come from all strata of society. This *attack-all move* turned out to have a tremendous drawing power.

USE OF SUNDAY MORNING WITNESSING PARTIES

1929 saw another avenue of drawing power come into use. Witnessing parties would begin visiting the homes of the people on Sunday morning between 10 and 12 a.m. This new avenue had this advantage: it quickly revealed who the unchurched people were. It also uncovered Christians who for one reason or another were playing truant from church attendance. As you read this, let it be a lesson to you. Do not stay home on Sunday mornings from church attendance, or J.W.s will get hold of you.

Many such Christians, who for one reason or another temporarily or sulkily stay at home from church attendance, lay themselves wide open to be drawn by Jehovah's Witnesses, who will endeavour to discover a grouse. Upon learning there is one, they will begin fastening onto you. Ezekiel 9: 1-3 will be quoted. Thus will begin a process of drawing you and marking you.

How wise it is for Christians not to let the sun go down over any wrong with their brother. If he waits, the devil will surely get into the act, and perhaps next Sunday the Jehovah's Witness will fasten onto you.

This Sunday-morning witnessing avenue has been, and is, drawing thousands of Christians and tens of thousands of unchurched ones into the NEW WORLD SOCIETY of Jehovah's Witnesses.

USE OF ROOMS FOR CONVENTION DELEGATES

As you read in my book *Thirty Years a WatchTower Slave*, we began as early as 1925 to solicit rooms for convention delegates in Magdeburg, Germany. The Watch Tower Society soon recognized this as a splendid avenue for horizontal drawing power. Today this has been methodized to a fine art. Now, wherever and whenever a city is selected to entertain a circuit, district or international convention, rooming committees are set up. Months before the arrival of the delegates teams of Jehovah's Witnesses solicit rooms from Christians and unchurched people for occupation by these convention delegates.

Householders are asked to rent spare rooms for a price for use by Christians. Many people are thus led into giving hospitality to thousands of Jehovah's Witnesses, veritably opening their doors wide to a people who deny the deity of Christ, even breaking bread with such (2 John 9–11).

As the assembly begins, delegates stream into the city. They occupy, like a fifth column, the very homes of Christians. Every evening they come home. Enthusiasm is generated for your benefit. The householder politely has to listen to the glowing reports of these delegates. Books are released during the assembly. Such are given free to the householder. He may even be inveigled, by sheer curiosity, to attend the public meetings of the assembly.

When the delegate leaves town he turns in the householder's name and address, including information as to the degree of his interest, on a back call slip to the local congregational servant.

During the 1958 International Assembly, held at Yankee Stadium in New York City, thousands of rooms were obtained in this manner. Now, shortly afterwards, the Watch Tower Society has a glowing report. They report that Jehovah's Witnesses had increased from the summer of 1958 to the winter of 1960 (January), in the greater New York area, from seventy-five to ninety-one units. I am not here talking of individuals. I am speaking of whole congregations. Remember *that* whenever rooms are solicited by Jehovah's Witnesses for assembly delegates from you or your neighbours who are unchurched Also note here the efficiency in the follow-up work. Large meetings have no value in winning souls for Christ unless the personal contacts enter into the picture. Apart from costing too much, in consecrated time and money, such large meetings in Christian circles do a great disservice in this, that they lull Christians into sleep, thinking that this is *evangelizing*. In Chapter III, I shall debunk that by fact.

However, here also is opportunity for the trained witness for Christ (Acts 1:8). If you know how to witness, evangelize and win souls, as this book will inform and train you, then *you* can use your home as a means to impress the gospel of Jesus Christ on such persistently, adroitly, effectively. Ponder on that as you proceed to equip and prepare yourself.

SEVEN STEPS

As the various avenues of drawing power began to produce larger groups who came unassimilated into the NEW WORLD SOCIETY, it became evident that people who came from so many different groups and strata, for so many different reasons, had only one thing in common. They wanted to gain life on earth between 1914 and Armageddon.

But how could so many divergent views otherwise held be synchronized? 1935 saw the beginning of the development of the seven-steps programme which would achieve a dual purpose: brainwash all former thinking and impregnate theocratic thinking in its place.

This seven-step programme, to be sure, began to be used world-wide in October 1938, when the THEOCRACY began. Most Jehovah's Witnesses today are not aware that such a programme is used on and through them.

Limit of space here prevents me from developing this programme for you at this time. But that is not necessary, as you will find it minutely and authoritatively described in *Thirty Years a Watch Tower Slave*. You have therein the entire set-up developed, adapted and explained.

Every Christian should have this information at his fingertips. This information, along with its sordid effects, should be shown and demonstrated to all Jehovah's Witnesses, one way or the other. No stones should be left unturned by you and your church to that end. There must be here no maudlin sentimentality displayed. This must be done firmly and with love. Often this alone will open their eyes. I have to date letters from all over the world from 7,918 converted J.W.s who have come free, which proves the value of such a presentation.

Once a person has been drawn, no matter how, into the grasp of the NEW WORLD SOCIETY, whether because of insecurity or by grousing, or on a Sunday morning, or by opening his home for delegates to a Watch Tower convention, he is taken through this seven-step programme. Coming through this process, his thinking has been totally changed. He is now become a dedicated Kingdom Publisher. He is now so different from what he once was, that not one of his former friends will recognize him to be the same person. What has been done to him? His thinking has been changed. The Watchtower gospel has solely dealt with his brain. It has never touched his heart and soul. This it cannot do. Therein lies the weakness of the so-called "gospel of the kingdom" preached by the Jehovah's Witnesses.

Only the gospel of Jesus Christ, bringing the power of faith in our Lord Jesus Christ and the righteousness of God into our hearts, can counteract the false gospel of the Jehovah's Witnesses. Reasonings will not do it. Engender faith in Jesus Christ in the heart of a Jehovah's Witness, and then observe how this power not only changes the J.W.s thinking, but also his heart and soul, bringing in a new birth. Faith in Jesus Christ changes everything: heart, soul, mind, subjection of the body, everything becomes new. It brings in a new birth.

PREACH THE GOSPEL OF JESUS CHRIST

Jehovah's Witnesses, thus trained, come to your doors preaching this so-called "gospel of the kingdom." Provocatively, they bring this false gospel to you in order to draw you into the NEW WORLD SOCIETY of Jehovah's Witnesses. How are you, a Christian, going to deal with them? If you decided to argue, or are unwittingly goaded into it, you will only pour fuel on the fiery zeal for the Theocracy.

But more important, as a Christian you are enjoined not to argue (Titus 3: 9). In 2 Timothy 2: 24–26 you are exhorted to be "gentle, patient, apt to teach." Christian, how can you exercise such patience?

When you open your doors to the knock of the Jehovah's Witness, let him make his presentation uninterrupted. As he observes you listening he may feel you are becoming interested

This will intensify his remarks. When he finishes on this intense note, he will expect you to react. Never make the mistake to wade in and argue with him. The moment you do that you walk right into his trap. In his presentation he has laid his premise, and if you come in on that you can never win. You will only lose the argument, and as you lose it you will become hot under the collar and "bang goes the door." Be wise; never argue at this point. Simply *ignore* what he has said. Leave his remarks dangling in mid-air. That will become very disconcerting to him.

Most Christians today are shocked by the appearance of heresies. But do not be. Listen to what the Apostle Paul said long ago: "for there must also be heresies among you, that they which are approved may be made manifest" (1 Cor. 11: 19). How can we manifest our being approved? By arguing? No. But by giving to such heretics what was given to us. What was that? To us, by someone, was delivered the gospel of Jesus Christ (1 Cor. 15: 1–3; Rom. 1: 16). So let us not cover this up, or be ashamed of it, or be goaded out of mentioning it by the pull of argument, but *confess* it to Jehovah's Witnesses to the exclusion of any satisfaction of argument we may get. Back up this invitation by telling them how you personally experienced the coming of the Lord Jesus into your heart by faith.

This frank testimonial statement on your part, in the place of rebuttal of their presentation, has at once a telling effect upon Jehovah's Witnesses (Acts 28: 31). In this manner you have, so to speak, in a sweep, taken the whole matter out of their hands and therefore out of the realm of argumentation which they had so cleverly set up, and placed it squarely upon the basis of witnessing. Who can argue with your confession of what the Lord Jesus means to you and how He came into your heart? That is not debatable. The Jehovah's Witness realizes it too, and shakes his head. Quite often he will leave it like that, and, thinking that you are touched in the head, will leave you. But think, if Jehovah's Witnesses got that kind of treatment in every Christian home what the accumulative effect would be? More so, if at the end of such a defence of the truth the Witness had to leave the field and, as the door closed, you began to bring his plight to the Lord in prayer, how proper that would be. After such a faithful witness for Christ which you just gave, if you back that up with prayer, such prayer will avail more than any argument of yours could have, as in this manner you invoke the Spirit of God. Watch, witness, and pray.

Always remember that the Master's voice, which still speaks out of the unaltered gospel of Jesus Christ, may at any time, at the nudge of the Holy Spirit, be heard by the Jehovah's Witnesses. Expose Jehovah's Witnesses continually to the gospel of Jesus Christ; yea; expose all men to it!

CASTING DOWN IMAGINATIONS

Often the same Jehovah's Witness will return. Your effective witness will have smarted him, and he will feel that he will have to set things straight. He will be equipped with a whole list of passages from the Bible, or a copy of a chocolate-coloured book named *Make Sure of All Things*. These texts are usually torn out of context, and are used in accordance with Watch Tower imaginations, which almost always are subtle and enterprising reasonings (Gen. 3: 1). If you let him, the Jehovah's Witness will weave scripture after scripture, taking you through the Bible on an imaginary trip. A sort of guided tour, showing you only what he wants you to see. They put this procedure as "running to and fro in the Bible to increase knowledge" (Dan. 12: 4). Your problem is *not* to permit them to run to and fro. In fact, slow them down to a crawl. Pin them down in their flight of Watch Tower imagination for their own good (2 Tim. 2: 25, 26). So be wise. At their mention of the first Scripture, stop them by saying, "Wait, I want to bring my Bible to the door." Upon returning you take command by asking, "May I have the first Scripture?" You look it up, then read it out aloud. But do not stop there. Continue reading the context. When finished, you ask for the next Scripture. After you have treated it in the same fashion, you ask for a third passage. After you have treated it in the same manner, ask for another. The Jehovah's Witness has not been trained in the niceties of resolving things, and will therefore not be able to stand this sort of treatment.

The Lord will bless you, for you have demonstrated to the Jehovah's Witnesses, better than any other kind of argument in its defence could ever have, HOW MUCH YOU THINK OF GOD'S WORD, THE BIBLE, in the loving manner in which you treated it. Primarily, you have given the Jehovah's Witness a lesson on how to "rightly divide the Word of Truth." You have pinned down his flight of imagination, exactly as you are taught in God's Word to do: "For though we walk in the flesh, we do not war after the flesh: (for the weapons of our warfare are not carnal, but mighty through God to the pulling down of strongholds;) *casting down imaginations*, and every high thing that exalteth itself against the knowledge of God, and bringing into captivity every thought of the obedience of Christ" (2 Cor 10: 3–5).

TWO ADMONITIONS (TITUS 3: 10)

Twice now you have dealt with a particular Jehovah's Witness. Should he return, which he often will for a third time, which is evoked by your manner of handling him in the first two encounters, how to acquit yourself a man in Christ? You know this cannot go on indefinitely. The above text puts a limit on your intercourse with a heretic.

You open the conversation this time. "Twice I have had your visit. I gave you my testimony, and have shown you how to read the Bible properly. But you return, and this puts a burden for you upon my heart. You have excited me to become concerned about you."

"What is your name?" you continue. "Mine is . . . So you are a Kingdom Publisher? How long have you been one?" If he replies, "three years," you know that he is still fanatically embued with indoctrination (the shorter the period a Jehovah's Witness has been brainwashed, the less likely you are to do him much good). On the other hand, you also know that he cannot be as formidable in ability as he would be if he had said "fifteen". Had he said "fifteen years", then you would know that he must have already experienced many disillusionments. So you have learned something important.

Then ask the next question, "How many hours do you put in each month in your worship from house to house with books?" If the witness should answer "seven hours", you can know by that he is not a very good Witness. He is supposed to worship this way at least as long as his company or national quota charts if he is a Company Publisher, and one hundred hours a month if he is a Pioneer. In this way you can gauge whom you have in front of you.

Now, make your main thrust. Ask, "Can I have your address?" "Why do you want my address?" the Witness will immediately ask. As a rule they do not like giving their addresses. You reply, "You have come here now three times. Your persistency has put a burden upon my heart. I feel the Lord wants me to help you. I do not want this to become a one-way street, with you doing all the work. You have come the first mile, asking me to come along with you. I am now impelled to go the second mile with you. That is why I want your address. I want to come and visit you at least three times, as you did me."

In most cases this takes the starch out of the Jehovah's Witnesses. Most J.W.s will thereafter never return to your home, because they will fear that if they do you would only persist in asking for their address. By doing it this way, behold how gracefully you have carried out Paul's instructions in Titus 3: 10, 11, "A man that is a heretic after the first and second admonition reject; knowing that he that is such is subverted (brainwashed), and sinneth, being condemned of *himself*." In refusing to give you his address, the Jehovah's Witness has stopped himself from coming again to see you.

PRACTICAL SUGGESTIONS IN DEALING WITH JEHOVAH'S WITNESSES

During this whole presentation I have taken into account all three possibilities in your meeting Jehovah's Witnesses. Notice, that we have here simplified the entire matter to (1) preaching the gospel; (2) using God's Word rightly; (3) causing a crisis in the encounter the third time. This reduces the area of conversation to the simplest level.

Everyone, knowing of this simple way, can cope with Jehovah's Witnesses. Of course, this has been done for two reasons. One, most so-called "laymen" are not capable of properly defending their faith. However, they can follow the above simple rules. Two, believe it or not, this weakness prevalent in present-day Christianity to witness ably for Christ, can in this instance be turned to advantage. In dealing with Jehovah's Witnesses who have been totally brainwashed, this simple way of witnessing is *the best way*.

At no time, be advised, accept anything printed from the Jehovah's Witness. Understand what their literature means

to them. They feel that it, their books, booklets and magazines, pamphlets and papers, are God's Word. They are
constantly assured that if they put just one piece of literature
into your home, however little, that sooner or later their visit
will have been a success. If you refuse to accept any literature
whatever, in a kind but firm manner, you do two things to
their thinking: (1) you accentuate a wide area of frustration;
(2) you startle them by your firmness not to have anything to
do with their literature. This often will soften them up for the
next Christian. Always remember, one of us alone cannot do
it. All of us working together, according to a pattern, can
do it, because the Holy Spirit will uphold the work. Just do
it right: no argument; no unfriendliness; firmness; gentleness;
always keeping in mind the three cardinal principles enunciated above.

However, not all Jehovah's Witnesses will refuse to give you
their address. Some may have been treated this way before
by some Christian, and at this stage may be ready to see what
in the world you will do, if and when you come to their home.
In fact, they have been taught by the Watch Tower Society
that no Christian is capable of defending his religion and
doctrines.

But do not be concerned about that. Remember just this
one over-riding fact. The Jehovah's Witness who gives you
his address *may be* saved. Thus, after the Witness has given
you his address and has left you, immediately go down upon
your knees and get the Lord into the matter. Ask him to
cleanse you to become a vessel through whom the Holy Spirit
can work. And then: GO TO WORK.

How? Take hold of my book, *Thirty Years a Watch Tower
Slave*, and study it very carefully. In it, for the first time, you
will find authentic information about Jehovah's Witnesses:
of how they have been dealt with by the Society; of what they
have lost; what makes them act in the way they do. Know
everything important about them. Once you know their
history, their weaknesses, what has been done with their
thinking, you will thereafter meet them knowing important
things about them. USE that information in facing them to
restrain you from wrong moves impelling you to move according to the above set plan.

The next step is to get hold of my most important book,
Into the Light of Christianity. A book like this could only be

written by someone who knows and has experienced both types of knowledge: the knowledge by reason (Rom. 1 : 19) employed by the Jehovah's Witnesses, and the knowledge of our Lord Jesus Christ (John 1 : 18) or the evangelical knowledge which can lead to salvation. It could not have been written by a Christian nor by a Jehovah's Witness who was just a Witness or a Company Servant.

As you prepare to visit the Jehovah's Witness whose address you obtained, be mindful of these three things: (1) you cannot have a Bible study with a Jehovah's Witness; (2) you cannot argue doctrines with a Jehovah's Witness; (3) you must not have a random conversation with a Jehovah's Witness. Taking these three points now in the reverse order:

(3). A random conversation is the strong point of a Jehovah's Witness. He does much more reading than you do, most likely, and his reading is done in Watch Tower literature. He gives the appearance of being well-informed, and can fasten on to any daily topic, which he will deftly turn into channels constantly becoming narrower, and before you know it he has you pinned. For that reason, never do anything whatever at random with a Jehovah's Witness. *Have a well-laid-out plan of procedure.*

(2). The doctrines Jehovah's Witnesses teach are upheld by reason, and are coloured with fine shades of interpretations. The "doctrines" once delivered to the saints are upheld by the Holy Spirit, and come by revelation and faith. They grow into your consciousness as your faith increases. You can't attain that sort of thing by arguing, so don't try.

(1). At one time Jehovah's Witnesses were taught to tear our Bibles apart, by having every salient scripture coloured with Watch Tower imaginations. Now, all of these Watch Tower imaginations have been incorporated into their NEW WORLD TRANSLATION OF THE HOLY SCRIPTURES. The moment you start a Bible study they will bring their version out, and in this way they will meet you on what appear to be Bible grounds. Nothing but damage can come to yourself here, so shun it.

If, then, random conversation, presentation of doctrines, and Bible study are out, what can you do to make your visit to the Jehovah's Witness fruitful?

Jehovah's Witnesses have one overriding weakness. They believe with all their hearts in book studies. That is how they were brainwashed: buying a book; being encouraged to read the book; then a home book study; then a kingdom hall book study, etc., etc., all seven steps.

When I was employed in training Kingdom Publishers as a Zoneservant I would study carefully the techniques of good salesmen. These become so completely sold on their product, and on spinning an eloquent tale about it, that this kind of action becomes second self with them. I found that I could sell more Watchtower books to such salesmen and businessmen dealing with the public than to any other group. Why? They were adept in using pressure on others by talking, fully knowing their product; and by the same token they would be so convinced of the effectiveness of this method that they themselves could be reached in the same manner. I held territories in the heart of the Manhattan business district when Company servant in New York City, and pioneer; I worked the Paramount building and the Times building and many other skyscrapers, and sold from thirty-five to fifty books a day by using this very same method on these people.

Jehovah's Witnesses are like such salesmen. If you come to their home, after they have given you their address, and you ask them to read together with you, and initially proceed to compare with them the doctrine of the deity of Christ by ostensibly checking the statements made from both sides in use of my book *Into the Light of Christianity*, they will accept it. It will challenge them. This book, written by one who for long years helped create procedures by which such threads were put together, unerringly touches the *chord finale*, and deftly begins unravelling the whole thing right before their eyes. The secret is, to start this study, and to keep it going through all the three chapters on the Deity. Then move backwards to the three chapters on Hell. Finally, take up the three chapters on the Soul. Your work, by the appearance of this book, has been made easy.

Your plan now is: from the moment a Witness appears at your door the first time, handle him exactly as suggested. If he returns the second time, which he will because you have challenged his faith in your first encounter, be sure to handle him as suggested, for only in that way will you tantalize him and his pride to come back a third time. If he returns the third time, then make your main thrust. If you fail here, do not worry. Someone else will get to him sooner or later. If you do not fail, and get his address, you are O.K. You have not taken a book from him, so he cannot start his seven-step programme on you or in an attempt give it up. You have not given him that opening. You see now how important it was not to have accepted literature? You have gotten his address by sticking to this plan. Now read carefully *Thirty Years a Watch Tower Slave*, then equip yourself with *Into the Light of Christianity*, and then go to work. You cannot lose. You have the plan, the book *Into the Light of Christianity*, the method and, above all, YOU HAVE THE TRUTH ON YOUR SIDE, and, having been led behind the scenes of the Watch Tower movement in *Thirty Years a Watch Tower Slave*, you now have compassion with Jehovah's Witnesses, and will therefore be able to "preach the truth in love" to them.

The development of the seven-step programme gave Jehovah's Witnesses a powerful set of tools to subvert millions. The development of this programme over four years will give you Christian the MEANS to undo its effects, and, more, to win brainwashed ones to Christ.

My second and more important book, *Into the Light of Christianity*, deals with the J.W. doctrines in the light of Scripture most effectively, and thus the battle is joined. It is no longer fought at the doors primarily, nor in the Watch Tower literature; now it is joined in the hearts of the Jehovah's Witnesses. Only by establishing a book study in *Into the Light of Christianity* will you be able to unravel error and resolve it with truth.

With the appearance of the bi-monthly *Converted Jehovah's Witness Expositor* we have prepared a regular medium to press it home—by equipping you, the Christian, with knowledge, know-how, method and techniques. Also, now you can subscribe for the *Expositor* right into the home of the Jehovah's Witness. There it will become a missionary.

Equip yourself, therefore, as soon as you have read this: (1) with several copies of *Thirty Years a Watch Tower Slave*; (2) several copies of *Into the Light of Christianity*; (3) a regular subscription to the *Converted Jehovah's Witness Expositor*.

May the Lord bless you as you go to work.

LESSON ONE

The Saga Of Personal Evangelism

Personal evangelism can come only in the wake of believing and coming to a new life, in the Saviour. Once the Christian is born again, and begins to grow in faith, in grace and truth, a personal relationship with Jesus Christ becomes possible.

The Lord Jesus is in heaven, and rules from there in the hearts of His people, by and through the Holy Spirit. That is "his rod (or sceptre) going forth from Zion" in which manner "He rules amidst His enemies".

The Lord is thus brought to live through the lips and the testimony of His disciples on earth, who, in giving such testimony, breathe this new life.

The power in this new life is not "the breath of life" we draw through our nostrils, but the power of the Holy Spirit given to every one of us (Acts 1 : 8). To the extent the Christian uses this power, to that extent he lives after the Spirit. This entire action spells out a WITNESS FOR CHRIST.

In this series of seven issues of Volume IV of *The Converted Jehovah's Witness Expositor*, entitled "CHRISTIANS: AWAKE!", there are seven training lessons: to wit: (1) "How to witness to Jehovah's Witnesses"; (2) "How to use truth versus error"; (3) "How to witness for Christ"; (4) "How to evangelize or make personal contacts"; (5) "How to win souls for Christ"; (6) "How to organize the TRAINING, TEACHING AND TELLING PLAN in a church"; (7) "How to organise group witnessing in a church".

To further pin-point the entire material, we have couched it into eight specific training lessons, of which this is the first. Four appear in chapter 2, HOW TO USE TRUTH VERSUS ERROR; the sixth follows chapter 4, the seventh follows chapter 5, and the eighth follows chapter 6.

HOW TO WITNESS FOR CHRIST

(a) Who alone can become a witness?
(b) Must every Christian become a responsible witness?
(c) What blessings are promised upon witnessing?

(*d*) What is the cost?

(*e*) What are the MUSTS in preparing to witness?

(*a*) WHO ALONE CAN BECOME A WITNESS?

Obviously, as you have read HOW TO WITNESS FOR CHRIST, you will realize that only those who are born again can witness about Jesus.

(*b*) MUST EVERY CHRISTIAN BECOME A RESPONSIBLE WITNESS?

The Bible shows that every one of us is his brother's keeper. John and other writers show that we "must love our neighbour". Moreover, read with profit here Ezekiel 33: 4–11. (Also study carefully at this stage chapter 5.)

(*c*) WHAT BLESSINGS ARE PROMISED UPON WITNESSING?

In Deuteronomy 10: 17–19 the Lord enjoins His love for the stranger. Ever and anon, the Lord has shown favour to the stranger. Often, when someone cannot prosper in his own country, and, emigrating to a new land, applies himself there, the Lord blesses him and he becomes well-to-do. This is especially true of the Christian who goes outside his church finding new people. How to do that is featured in "practical suggestions on witnessing" in lesson 3: How to Witness for Christ. Study that here.

(*d*) WHAT IS THE COST?

Wherever the gospel of Jesus Christ is preached, there is opportunity to win souls. After all, it is the "sceptre which goes forth from Zion". However, the moment souls are being saved Satan steps in, either to cause division, or to deflect those preaching the gospel.

As you go about witnessing, either in the neighbourhood or among your acquaintances, or from house to house, you will soon draw down upon yourself ridicule, and in time opposition. Can you take that? That is the cost.

Look upon the Lord, whom you are following. He too was ridiculed, He suffered; yes, even died. How did He accomplish that? Paul says "Looking unto Jesus, the author and finisher of our faith; who for the joy that was set before Him endured the cross, despising the shame, and is set down at the right hand of God" (Heb. 12: 2).

In other words, be aware, Christian: the moment you become a witness for Christ is the moment you will be contradicted, laughed at, ridiculed, slandered, and finally may even be killed. Knowing that, trust in the Lord and then set your sights high, look straight at Jesus, remember while you are looking that in Him you will become an overcomer of the world and of the devil and, as an overcomer, you will enter into heaven. Think about Stephen, the first man on earth (after Jesus) who became a martyr. He was like you, a layman. He was not an apostle or a pastor. But look how he did overcome! He witnessed for Christ, and then looking straight to heaven observe what were the last things he saw and said; "And they stoned Stephen, calling upon God, and saying, Lord Jesus, receive my spirit" (Acts 7: 59).

If you look upon Jesus, and are animated by the joy of being His servant, and have been found worthy to become a witness for Christ, you shall never see nor feel the persecution. So set your sights high, be confident and be fearless!

(e) WHAT ARE THE MUSTS IN PREPARING TO WITNESS?
1. Prepare yourself to become a clean vessel.
2. Have a definite statement in mind.
3. Prepare your outward appearance.
4. Cultivate the right attitude,
5. Look for an opening; when it presents itself, step in firmly.
6. Make sure of a reason to return.

1. *Prepare yourself to become a clean vessel.*

Nothing is more important than for you to realize that the power of the Holy Spirit cannot operate in you if you are unclean. Secret sins, wrong thoughts, many reasons in our lives, may mitigate against the working of the Holy Spirit. Come to the Lord in prayer. Pray fervently for the Lord to reveal your secret sins, and then ask for forgiveness. Continue asking the Lord to steady you, with assurance that you are in His hands, doing His work. Then rest confidently in faith.

2. *Have a definite statement in mind.*

Never go witnessing without knowing exactly what you want to say. Thus prepare yourself to a definite statement. Make sure you know it. An outline is the best method. From an outline etched into your mind you can become extempore in such a way that is conducive to your conduct. Circumstances, people, occasions, will evoke different approaches and words, but the outline will be the same. Once you grasp that, you will have poise. Poise is calmness and certainty that you can handle any situation. Trust in the Lord.

3. *Prepare your outward appearance.*

To the two ingredients for poise, preparing yourself to be a clean vessel and with the outline of a definite statement riveted into your mind, you must now add the third ingredient: that is outward cleanliness.

Paul said, "Cleanliness is next to godliness." Clean in body, properly groomed, your appearance will add confidence and also appeal. Many doors will open. Nothing hidden will bother you, because you know you have the Lord's approval, know what you are going to say and know that you make a clean appearance.

4. *Cultivate the right attitude.*

Equipped with poise, go out willing to accommodate ALL men. How? Find the widest area for agreement in every contact. You are there to help YOUR contact. His views matter. You have to break down the barriers. Attitude alone will do it.

Paul said he was "a Greek unto a Greek", etc. Why? So that he could win men for Christ.

Recently I came to a door and knocked. A man opened and I said, "Good morning. I am here to witness to you that I am a Christian. I would very much like to have a chat with you about Christianity." I was interrupted . . . "I am a Catholic. We are Christians, and I go to church and therefore do not see how we could discuss this. . . ." Here I interrupted, "Oh, you are Catholic. Catholic, does this not mean universal? Why yes. Universal, that is what Christianity is— certainly we two should have a lot in common." While I said that, generating an expansive attitude, this man's mouth opened and the lips hung open, completely amazed. Finally he said, "If you feel that way about it, come on in."

For fifteen minutes we compared our faith. An amiable conversation led to friendliness and, as a result, we became better men in our thinking because of it.

5. *Look for an opening; when it presents itself, step in firmly.*

Remember, your entering into a conversation is only the beginning. Spiritual language comes only into full bloom when a meeting-point has been reached, caused by your discerning a spiritual need in your contact.

Around such a need, then, must a relationship be based, designed to enlarge the area of need on the one hand, and the means to overcome it on the other. Mere conversation suffices not. You must begin to "light the spirit of man, which is the candle of the Lord" (Prov. 20: 27). The lesson dealing with "HOW TO MAKE THE PERSONAL CONTACT" will show you how to carry the operation out (page 76).

6. *Make sure of a reason to return.*

However, in order ever to get to the stage of a concerted endeavour to "light the spirit of man", you must initially win approval to return. That is your immediate concern. Either secure such an invitation by not being able to answer a question put, promising to look it up and returning with the answer in a week, or, by propounding a question yourself, which could not be answered at the moment, promising to return with facts. Or, ask permission to come by and pick the person up to come to a Bible study. Many such possibilities can be conjured up by you. Never come back just because you were passing by. Definitely set the time and the reason.

You will profit greatly at this stage to read carefully chapters five and six.

CHAPTER II

HOW TO USE TRUTH VERSUS ERROR

Men in general—and Jehovah's Witnesses in particular—have three kinds of goods. The first is the external; such as gold, silver, money, clothing, land, houses, servants, wives, children, etc. The second kind is the physical and personal goods; such as health, strength, beauty, disposition of members, aptitude of body and senses, reputation and honour. Then we find the third which is spiritual and internal; such as knowledge, virtue, love, faith.

All of these which I have mentioned (and which I will even more vividly demonstrate in my coming book *Is the New World Society of Jehovah's Witnesses Christian?*), are being harnessed into slave-like service.

I, William J. Schnell, erstwhile occupied in Magdeburg, Germany, and for sometime in Bethel of Brooklyn, N.Y., former Zoneservant, for a while special confidential representative of Judge Rutherford in the Midwest, special pioneer, pioneer and Kingdom Publisher, and also twenty-one years in full-time service in the NEW WORLD SOCIETY OF JEHOVAH'S WITNESSES, do humbly confess that during all that time, I was a sinner. In these sins, I had enjoyed the full approval of the Watchtower Society.

As soon as I forsook this association of sinfulness, immediately there fell upon me the full fury of

THE BURNING HATRED OF THE NEW WORLD SOCIETY

When my first book (*Thirty Years a Watch Tower Slave*) appeared, I knew that I would be dealt with in total silence until the effects of what I had done had been gauged.

As the book aroused Jehovah's Witnesses, it forced the Watchtower Society into a miscalculation. Believing me to be a sorehead with an axe to grind, the Society opined that I would begin to draw followers after me. This had been the pattern followed in the formation of the eleven existing Watchtower sects.

One of the agents in the inner group of the Society, a Mr. McMillan, thereupon wrote, *A Manner of Faith: A Joyous Lifetime Service with Jehovah's Witnesses.* Because of this, there was created two views: Mine, in *Thirty Years a Watch Tower Slave,* depicting Watch Tower service as "slavery"; and Mr. McMillan's, depicting it as "a joyous lifetime of service with Jehovah's Witnesses." This appeared to say: TAKE YOUR PICK. It produced a stand-off which for a while successfully did undercut my book with Jehovah's Witnesses.

Cutting me off in this manner from Jehovah's Witnesses' support, they hoped that I would soon be forgotten. But the Lord intervened . . . I was not a sorehead who had an axe to grind. I had come to a conviction of my many sins on that morning of April 18, 1952, and had repented them. The Lord had graciously sent the ability to "believe" into my heart. That morning, I was saved!

The Lord's grace began to work in my heart, and instead of being bitter, I became a person dedicated to help win Jehovah's Witnesses for Christ. Churches and denominations sensed my burden and gave me a magnificent platform upon which I commanded audiences in the aggregate of 665,000 persons in four years. Christian booksellers stepped in with missionary zeal and spread my book (as I hope they will continue to promote my second and more important book, *Into the Light of Christianity*). As a result, men and women found salvation and to date, I possess letters from 7,918 Jehovah's Witnesses who have come to Christ.

Because of this widespread success, *Into the Light of Christianity* was penned. This book is the true antidote to engineered brainwashing of Jehovah's Witnesses. Today in hundreds of homes, it is already clearing heresy out of the minds of Jehovah's Witnesses and is healing their souls of that malady. Already many Christians are using it as a textbook in conducting bookstudies with infected ones.

Since the appearance of *Into the Light of Christianity*, the battle for the souls of Jehovah's Witnesses has been joined. Now the Watch Tower "High Command" knows that a tool has been produced which Christians can use to undo the damage that has been done in the minds of Jehovah's

Witnesses by the Watchtower Organization. To discredit me
(its author) with pastors and churches, it permits an undercover
campaign of character assassination in the midst of Jehovah's
Witnesses which today has reached its zenith in Canada,
Germany, England and South Africa and is spreading all over
the world. It is, of course, designed to make me *persona non
grata* to Christianity.

I am being accused of everything within the area of human
relations from lying to adultery. Of course, you know the old
saying, "Where there's smoke, there's fire". Do not discount
this. These people are not discounting it. I knew it was
coming when I wrote *Thirty Years a Watch Tower Slave,* and
pointed it out in chapter 21 of that book ("Coming Out of the
Labyrinth of Watchtower Slavery"). Please read it at this
stage. For that reason, I do not discount it.

You are given there in chapter 21 an inkling that I knew
I was a sinner all those thirty years of Watch Tower service, I
knew I badly needed a Saviour and forgiveness. My whole
life and work inside of the NEW WORLD SOCIETY OF JEHOVAH'S
WITNESSES had become unbearable. I had become seriously
affected, morally and spiritually, as the pendulum of beha-
viour-pattern swung from the super-holiness of "Russellites"
to the laxity of the "Rutherford Era".

All of us, without a personal Saviour, were tarred with the
same brush of sinfulness and iniquity. During all this time
in which I purportedly committed all of these "atrocities"—
as a Jehovah's Witness recently described them in writing to
the so-called "Life Messengers, Inc."—I was a servant in
good standing with the Society.

They still wallow in the cesspool of this *clean Organization,*
and neatly dressing things up, today they spread these tales
about me concerning my former life. But I, William J. Schnell,
once a Watch Tower servant, am now in peace of heart and
joy by the grace of our Lord Jesus.

While travelling in your midst, Christians, have you ever
heard me vilify, belittle or downgrade Jehovah's Witnesses?
No matter what they now do and say, I pledge and pray
that the Lord may give me strength to "turn the other
cheek".

With the forthcoming appearance of my most important
book *Is The New World Society of Jehovah's Witnesses Christian?,*
this sort of thing will reach its crescendo. Like it or not, I

now must move all the way in self-degradation from the beginning of the description made in chapter 21 of my book *Thirty Years a Watch Tower Slave*, because this phase of battle concerns the third kind of human goods, to wit: spiritual and internal goods (such as knowledge, virtue, love, faith).

I had tried the approach of an outreach of love and kindness to undo Watch Tower error in the misuse of these human goods. Many Jehovah's Witnesses have seen these errors and have come free, thereby saving their souls.

But it appears that errors of the spirit make for hardness and since the Watch Tower Society refuses to enter upon a discussion as openly as I have in attacking it and now permits the issue to be obscured by allowing gossip about my former character to enter in, like it or not, I have only one recourse.

As a Christian witness, I must now further humiliate myself and parade before the world my former sinfulness while I was an honoured Watch Tower servant. In displaying this sinfulness I hope to draw Jehovah's Witnesses out of themselves, out of their proud Watch Tower stance and into a realization of their sinfulness, so that they can come to see their need of a Saviour.

There is only one proper way to react to slander as a witness for Christ. In witnessing to what the Lord Jesus did for me, by displaying my former sinfulness, I also show that this was common practice amongst us. I am, after all, a product of the NEW WORLD SOCIETY OF JEHOVAH'S WITNESSES.

I do not like to do this but obviously the Lord wants all of my pride to be vanquished. I am no better than were men of God in the past in similar circumstances. Such men often had to display their sinfulness in the pages of the Bible in order to lead others to repentance. Others had to commit unusual and outlandish things (as you read in Hos. 1: 2, 3; Ezek. 4: 2–7; Jer. 27: 1. 2).

In this manner the Lord pointed through His Word how I must behave. My former life was sinful; I cannot defend it. But in further humbling myself, Watchtower rumours and gossip will lose their force and sting, for in my present state I fully agree with the apostle Paul: "What things were gain to me, those I counted loss for Christ. Yea doubtless, and I count all things but loss for the excellency of the knowledge of Christ

Jesus my Lord, for whom I have suffered the loss of all things, and do count them but dung, that I may win Christ" (Phil. 3: 7, 8).

In the light of this resolve, if Jehovah's Witnesses want to wallow in the "dung" of my Watchtower past and refuse to look upon the joyful Christian present, I will be forced to counteract by displaying the stench of it to all the world.

My story—my "open-and-aboveboard" attack and exposé of the NEW WORLD SOCIETY OF JEHOVAH'S WITNESSES—has obviously forced a total change in the Society's tactics. For the first time in its 85 years of checkered existence, it has had to go on record and into print—black on white—to produce its history. This history which appeared in 1959 is titled, *Jehovah's Witnesses in the Divine Purpose.*

This book is a colossal whitewash! Nevertheless, it is a concrete basis for me upon which to operate in debunking the Watchtower heresy. Thus, my coming book, *Is the New World Society of Jehovah's Witnesses Christian?* must prove one thing; namely, that the NEW WORLD SOCIETY is not Christian. It is a world-wide heresy, a superb Organization, even perhaps a whole new world; but in erecting it, and in finding it, I will show that its followers have lost their souls.

For the first time in its existence the entire NEW WORLD SOCIETY OF JEHOVAH'S WITNESSES will be forced into the defensive. The battle is now joined. It will be fierce! It will be without quarter! It will become ugly and as it progresses many may be frightened away because of the issue—perhaps even all! Because somebody has to assume the offensive, I am going on record here that I, fully trusting in the Lord, shall continue to wage the battle even if I have to fight the error alone.

Although the Lord has given many new friends to me, I have lost sisters, mother, nephews and nieces, who today will have nothing to do with me. But graciously, hand in hand toward freedom, the Lord permitted my wife to come out with me. Since 1952, He has made both of our lives completely satisfying by His forgiveness of our sins. Thus, we both rededicate ourselves to Him and His service to Christian witnessing.

After all is said and done, it is not too difficult—once the Lord Jesus has come into our hearts—to further humble ourselves in the flesh. It could still be worse; we could still be called upon to follow the example of Samson's last act in life in the Philistine temple.

INTO THE LIGHT OF CHRISTIANITY

In 1959, the very year of the "great whitewash" of the NEW WORLD SOCIETY OF JEHOVAH'S WITNESSES (with the appearance of the history titled, *Jehovah's Witnesses in the Divine Purpose*), there came the antidote to Watch Tower proselytising.

Into the Light of Christianity is a tool. When in the hands of a trained Christian, it can debunk Watch Tower brainwashing of Jehovah's Witnesses; it can also heal their minds of heretical malady.

Following are four training lessons that will teach you how to effectively use *Into the Light of Christianity*.

LESSON TWO

SUGGESTIONS TO CHRISTIANS WHO DESIRE TO WIN BACK THEIR JEHOVAH'S WITNESS FRIENDS AND RELATIVES TO CHRIST

Often Christians write asking me to forward the name and address of a converted Jehovah's Witness so that they can use such a one to win back their friends or relatives to Christ.

There are two valid reasons why, since January 1, 1961, I can no longer accede to such requests:

(1) In a number of cases, because false brethren had found out what they were doing, these converted Jehovah's Witnesses have been exposed to unrelenting and severe persecution.

(2) If you have a burden and concern for such lost souls, then you are the logical person to undertake the job. The very fact that you have a burden is proof that the Lord is working on your heart, doing a work in and through you to win such a soul. It is the same Holy Spirit, who called Philip to go over to the chariot of the eunuch of Ethiopia, that is unctioning you. Heed the call! Trust the Lord! Prepare yourself!

There are nine wonderful steps that you now can employ to overcome the seven-step brainwashing that the Jehovah's

Witness has undergone. Where only a few years ago Christians saw no other recourse open than to slam the door and have nothing further to do with the Jehovah's Witness, the Lord now has wonderfully provided them with weapons which are spiritual in nature, embracing methods and techniques and "know-how", and most important of all, with a special type of literature. This literature copes successfully with this problem. Already, because of it 7,918 Jehovah's Witnesses—that we know of—out of some 108 lands, have come to Christ.

All of this raises positive hopes for your dear friends and relatives to come free of this heresy. Recently, *Herald of His Coming*, in a desire to be helpful, graciously advertised our work and literature free of charge. As a result of this, there have come hundreds of letters from Christians telling the revealing story of the great missionary work carried on in these Christian homes which I never dreamed was so pronounced. So far, letters from Christians evoked by this advertisement inform me that 172 J.W.'s were won for Christ by them at their doors, using this new type of literature put out by us. Just think of it! One woman reports already helping eight J.W.'s to Christ in subsequent bookstudies by use of *Into the Light of Christianity*.

All of this is making this one fact quite evident: In Jehovah's Witnesses, the Christian has a *world-wide missionary field* in which to work. Jehovah's Witnesses are zealous for their error. There is nothing lukewarm about them. They are hot. For that reason, if persistently and lovingly approached with the Gospel of Jesus Christ and the Word of God, they can be excited to come to the Lord Jesus. It is easier to convert them than it would be to transform a cold worldling. They *do believe* that the Bible is God's Word. Here is where they are vulnerable. By coming in the name of the Lord, i.e., by using the Scriptures, you can show them *how rightly to divide the Word of God*. If you truly are serious in your query to us to win these souls for Christ, then acquaint yourself thoroughly with the nine steps that follow. Plan and prepare to use them.

NINE STEPS TO WIN J.W.'S FOR CHRIST

(1) INVOKE PRAYERS

Prayer releases your burden before the Lord. If you persist in fervent, constant prayer, you will become spiritually attuned to your problem, especially as you begin to acquaint yourself with the special literature and techniques to deal with the J.W. Also, having become a good tree in Christ, you will want to do good to them.

"Love your neighbour" will be written in love in your heart and your burden for these lost souls will grow to a point where you will have to make a move to help. You are your brother's keeper, you know. Ezekiel 33: 7, 8 enjoins you, fellow Christians, to care.

As you pray for guidance, you will be watching where you can help in physical matters dealing with the external and intermediate goods of your J.W. neighbour, in order to come to grips with the internal human goods of the Jehovah's Witness.

Finally, you will enlist all your Christian friends, starting with the Pastor, to pray for these specific persons whom you are undertaking to win. Remember, your burden for them *is your call*. Follow it with complete abandon. "The prayer of the righteous availeth much" comes here into proper use.

(2) PREPARE YOURSELF

First, subscribe for the *Converted Jehovah's Witness Expositor* which is today the hallmark for effective soul-winning in the missionary work amidst Jehovah's Witnesses. Read it carefully.

Second, obtain my book *Thirty Years a Watch Tower Slave*. Read it thoroughly, marking points of importance to you. In this manner, you will learn important things about Jehovah's Witnesses; such as their thinking and their background.

Third, buy and read my second and more important book, *Into the Light of Christianity*. Here is your finest tool. Use it painstakingly as a textbook for a bookstudy with Jehovah's Witnesses. Meanwhile, learn to emulate its techniques.

Israel was commanded to treat the stranger squarely and the stranger in Israel was promised a blessing from the Lord (Deut. 10: 18, 19). The Lord has ever since blessed strangers. Often someone who could not prosper in his own country would emigrate to a strange land. There the Lord's blessings would become operative, and this same person would prosper. More than elsewhere is this true in Christian circles, for if "we go outside of the camp" (where we are strangers) to win lost souls for Christ, the Lord will mightily prosper us. There is a blessing on this. I encourage all Christians, not only to go out into strange places other than their own churches to find lost souls, but also to accord the best that we have; i.e., to bring the Gospel of Jesus Christ and Word of God to the strangers (Jehovah's Witnesses—for that is what they call themselves, or Watch Tower literature calls them), as Deuteronomy 10: 19 shows.

(3) USE DRAWING OUT FIRST

As you pray, have others pray for your Jehovah's Witness friend who considers himself a stranger to you and for you. When you read my books you will begin to know important facets about your friend's thinking. You will have absorbed this important information. You yourself will have been thoroughly reassured about the excellency of Christian doctrines over those of the Jehovah's Witness. Studying *Into the Light of Christianity* will give you that reassurance. You are now equipped to move in positively. You will no longer negatively attack the J.W. because he teaches error. Now you will uphold and defend the truth positively.

(a) Excite your J.W. friend to read *Thirty Years a Watch Tower Slave.* If he promises to read it, lend it to him for a week. At the end of the week, come back and then let him react. Let him blow off all the steam he wants to.

(b) How can you excite him for sure? Approach him in a humble manner and diplomatically say, "I have obtained this book written by a converted Jehovah's Witness and am puzzled about it. I know you might be able to help me. I want to leave it with you so you can read it. In a week I shall come back to get it and your views. Will you do this for me?" (After all you are his former friend or relative and you can rightfully impose on him this way.) It never fails, Christian, if you do it exactly this way. Do not take a chance by doing it in another way.

(4) FORCE "WRESTLING OF GOD'S WORD" BEFORE YOU

Coming back now to get his reaction, he will tear the book to pieces. He will attack me as being disfellowshipped, a traitor, liar, cheat, insane, adulterer, Judas, adventurer, thief, etc. Let him! Follow immediately once he is through (we both can turn the other cheek as we are out to win him for Christ—never forget that) with the instructions in "Preach the Gospel of Jesus Christ" (see chapter one). Give him all the time he wants to get everything off his chest. When he is through, forget what he has said and ignore it in full. Follow through on the instructions by presenting Christ and your own personal testimony. As soon as this is done, leave immediately and ask him to visit you.

(a) Wait a week for this visit to materialize. If he comes, he will have many scripture passages to show you. It is here you want to use the instructions in "Casting Down Imaginations" (see chapter one).

(b) Should he not come in one week, you return to him, remembering "If Mohammed will not come to the mountain, then let the mountain come to Mohammed". Provoke him gently by saying, "I have returned to see whether you have thought about my invitation to accept Christ as your personal Saviour." That will do it! He will go for his scripture passages and you begin to use the instructions you find in chapter one.

(5) START A BOOKSTUDY

If he visited you in the last described stage, you will have forced him to go home with conscience trouble. He will now *have* to return. If he does, use those portions of "Practical Suggestions Dealing with Jehovah's Witnesses" that you find in the first chapter.

(a) If you had to go back to his house, then use these instructions in this way: "I know from what you said that we are miles apart in our doctrines. I know you practice bookstudies. Let us have such a bookstudy now. We can use for a change this book *Into the Light of Christianity*. Here are the chapters on the Deity of Christ, where we differ most." Thereupon, sit down without invitation; as a suggestive move, open two copies of the book dealing with the Deity (there are three chapters), and ask him to get his Bible and helps. By doing this you conjure up the vista in his mind that he can have his way after all.

If he had returned, then start out right away with his Bible and helps. Do it this way: Read a paragraph; then look up all scripture passages—both quoted and cited—you and he alternating in hunting them up and reading them. Keep him busy. Then ask him questions; discuss answers. Even if you do not agree, move on; read the next paragraph. Stay no more than one hour. Do not let the study deteriorate into a long aftermath-conversation. Be businesslike; you are there to excite a soul for Christ, not to discuss the weather or Aunt Minnie's lumbago. Close the study with a prayer; make an appointment for the next study.

(*b*) Should the study continue through the three chapters on the Deity, go to the chapters on "Hell", and then to the chapters on the "Soul".

(*c*) Should it not continue . . .

(6) USE OUTSIDERS

There are different ways that you can get outsiders into the picture after you have failed. Read carefully at this stage chapters 4 or 5. Select one approach which seems appropriate to you.

(7) GOAL OF OUTSIDERS: BOOKSTUDY

Pursuing an approach as selected, let your outside helper move in gradually, slowly introducing *Into the Light of Christianity*—particularly on the subject of the Deity—as a textbook for the bookstudy.

(8) KEEP YOUR RELATIONSHIP OPEN AND FRIENDLY

While all this is going on, stay on friendly terms. Go out of your way to be nice. Be helpful; do little things for him. However, never mention the visits of your outside helper to his home that are now in progress. Press in on him by being kind, helpful, doing for him the things that he cannot do for himself. Make him love you. Slowly you will win him by acts of kindness done in the flesh and as you succeed he will requite subconsciously by keeping the study with your outside helper going. You are now pressing in on him in the spirit through the bookstudy conducted by your outside helper, and pressing in on him in the flesh by your acts of kindness; and all the while you and your outside helper are working, the congregation beginning with the Pastor is pressing in on his behalf with the Lord. You have wonderful results awaiting you. Just believe, pray and witness.

(9) SUBSCRIBE FOR A GIFT SUBSCRIPTION FOR THE "CONVERTED JEHOVAH'S WITNESS EXPOSITOR"

Human nature being what it is; the devil working as he does; and often the Lord's time to draw your friend or relative to Christ not having come as yet; you should still patiently continue friendly relations. Stay burdened for him in prayer—do not give up. Wait upon the Lord for it will make it easier for you spiritually. You can show this outwardly at this stage by subscribing for a gift subscription for the *Converted Jehovah's Witness Expositor*. From then on, we will take over by joining you as the pages of the *Converted Jehovah's Witness Expositor* come into his home every two months. It then becomes a Missionary.

Evangelizing and soul-winning is exacting work and you will succeed only if you use them correctly and unselfishly. Spend at least as much time with those whom you aspire to win for Christ, as the Jehovah's Witnesses do with them in subverting them.

LESSON THREE

How to Combat the False J.W. Doctrine: "Hell is the Grave"

This false doctrine is used by J.W.s as a spearhead against historic Christianity in an aggressive manner. The Watchtower Society has trained J.W.s to think of Hell as the grave, and has brainwashed all vestiges of the true Bible doctrine out of their minds.

In making J.W.s so positive and aggressive about this false doctrine, it has succeeded at the doors of Christians, alas, all too often. WHY? In the main there is great apathy in Christian, as well as unchristian circles, about the Bible doctrine, that HELL IS A PLACE OF ETERNAL PUNISHMENT AND TORMENT. The flesh does not like this doctrine.

Thus, the positive attack by J.W.s on this Bible doctrine finds most humans of the twentieth century quite willing to say nothing. The tragedy is, that we humans are created with a remarkable adaptability If we hear something often enough, even the grossest error, and do not earnestly contend against it, our minds will gradually tolerate such error. If pressed, we may finally accept the error as truth. Flesh generates reason, and reason generates reasonings, and in this manner we establish plausibility of error.

The best defence against such erosion is to EARNESTLY CONTEND FOR THE TRUTHS ONCE DELIVERED TO THE SAINTS.

In order to contend for such a doctrine, we must believe

it! In order to believe it, we must ascertain from where it came. At the outset, it is very important for us to remember that the Christian doctrine of Hell being a place of eternal punishment and torment is not a doctrine of man. It is Christ's doctrine (Mark 9: 43–48; Matt. 25: 41). The prophets of old already taught it at the behest of the Holy Spirit (Isa. 66: 24). The apostles taught it (2 Thess. 1: 9). As we read of it, we gradually will come to accept it in faith, and not by reason.

But the Witness's attack is one by reason—how can you counter that? KNOW what the Lord Jesus says about it; what the prophets said about it; what the apostles said about it; and what the Christian Church teaches on it. That is very important.

Since most Christians do not know how Jehovah's Witnesses came by the processes of reasonings generated for them, not by the Lord, the prophets and the apostles, but by reason of the flesh, it is important for them to see this. That is why my book *Into the Light of Christianity* becomes so important to both Christians and Jehovah's Witnesses.

Are you serious about winning Jehovah's Witnesses for Christ? Yes? Then learn to defend ably that the Bible doctrine of Hell is a place of eternal punishment in torment. Also learn about the pitfalls of reason raised by the Jehovah's Witnesses.

Take the following steps:

(1) Obtain a copy of my book *Into the Light of Christianity*.
(2) Read carefully the chapter "Historic Christian Doctrine: Hell is a Place of Eternal Punishment."
(3) Look up all the scripture passages proving and clarifying it.
(4) Mark these passages in the sequel presented.
(5) Re-study that chapter, once again.
(6) Now read carefully chapter 7, "'Hell is the Grave', say Jehovah's Witnesses and Other Cultists."
(7) Look up their scripture passages—mark them.
(8) Proceed now to read and carefully study chapter 8: "Which is True: Hell is a Place of Eternal Punishment in Torment, or Hell is the Grave?"
(9) Here you are presented with the rudiments of spiritual warfare. The entire chapter works on this scriptural principle:

"For though we walk in the flesh, we do not war after the flesh. For the weapons of our warfare are not carnal, but mighty through God to the pulling down of strongholds; casting down imaginations, and every high thing that exalteth itself against the knowledge of God, and bringing into captivity every thought to the obedience of Christ."

Notice the way it is done?

(a) Use of spiritual weapons—statements made for us about a doctrine by Jesus, the prophets and the apostles.

(b) A stronghold in reason is a proof, or a line of argument. You pull it down, first by reading the proof offered, then by reading the *entire* context out of which the passage was taken. You destroy the cohesion by following it up, then travelling on with what the Lord, the prophets and the apostles said. In this manner, you cast out the imagination of the flesh generated by reason, and by following through in this instance, by showing how great a sacrifice God brought for our sin by sending, killing and resurrecting His only begotten Son, in order to overcome the very real destiny of sin, death and eternal damnation we faced. You have made their thinking thus captive in Christ.

That is the way *Into the Light of Christianity* is written. You will learn how to use it, by very carefully reading, studying and then applying the chapter 8: "Which is True: Hell is a Place of Eternal Punishment in Torment, or Hell is the Grave?"

In *Into the Light of Christianity* you have a wonderful textbook on a heresy and on how to overcome it.

Believing in a gospel by reason, Jehovah's Witnesses value the written page immensely. They believe in bookstudies. That is their strong point. But also their weak point.

This positive attack on the Christian doctrine HELL IS A PL. CE OF ETERNAL PUNISHMENT AND TORMENT by use of their doctrine HELL IS THE GRAVE is formidable only if you let it go without defending your Bible doctrine.

The moment you are prepared, and KNOW what the Bible doctrine on Hell is, from that moment the J.W. attack becomes a weakness. For reason must flee faith. Your faith in believing what Jesus, the prophets and apostles said about Hell, will give you the edge from the moment you open your mouth.

Being mindful of the importance of the printed page and

bookstudy to J.W.s, immediately invite them to a bookstudy in *Into the Light of Christianity* chapters 6, 7 and 8.

How to do it?

(1) Sit down, have your Bibles ready, open your copy and the spare one for the J.W.

(2) Read the first paragraph aloud.

(3) Hunt up all scriptures whether quoted or cited. Have the J.W. read one, you the other.

(4) Ask questions—discuss the paragraph—never argue.

(5) Even if you do not agree, read the next paragraph—do the same.

(6) Keep the meeting going for one hour. Stop. End with prayer. Make an appointment for another meeting.

(7) Study all three chapters in this manner, if you can.

THE IMPORTANT THING IS . . .

(a) The system of study. It is this system that was used by Jehovah's Witnesses to brainwash the person studying with you. By following it, you are applying it in reverse, and eventually will bring the thinking of the J.W. back to his pre-brainwashed condition.

(b) Friendly studious atmosphere must be maintained at all times. No arguments, nor unfriendliness.

(c) Constant use of the Bible in looking up and checking every scripture, gradually lifts the Word of God out of the milieu of contention and replaces it to the source; a food and the working for the Holy Spirit.

Thus carefully follow this line, everywhere at all times. It will succeed if you use the printed page with it, plus the Word of God. The ideal here for Jehovah's Witnesses at least, is *Into the Light of Christianity*.

LESSON FOUR

How to Explain the Doctrine of the Soul

"Man is a soul" teach the Jehovah's Witnesses. How do they come to this conclusion?

While Holy Writ says: "Let us make man in our image, after our likeness . . ." (Gen. 1 : 26), Jehovah's Witnesses say,

"Man is like a beast, goes to the grave like a beast" (Eccles. 3: 18–20).

Both of the above statements are scriptural, but both are taken out of context. Do they produce a paradox?

The first passage, Genesis 1: 26, speaks of the creation of man in the likeness and image of God, while the second passage, Ecclesiastes 3: 18–20, speaks of man's dissolution which, because of sin and death, is like that of a beast.

In Genesis 2: 7, we see the execution of what Genesis 1: 26 projects: "And the Lord God formed man of the dust of the ground and breathed into his nostrils the breath of life; and man became a living soul."

The Hebrew word translated "breath of life" here is plural, and means "breath of lives".

Observe—man's body, or his flesh, was not created; it was formed. Man's inner life or spirit was breathed into his nostrils with the mouth of God, or into existence, or was created out of God.

Man is thus a dual-natured creature, with a body and a soul. Unlike the beast, man is an individuality which has an eternal identity. *That* is his likeness with God.

An identity can only be established and manifested by a pair of likes, as we say, "identical twins". In order to have an identity at all, man is a pair—inner and outer man, or body and soul. Disrupt these and the whole man dies; i.e., he loses his likeness with God—he becomes dead to God in this manner of disruption or dissolution.

This is wonderfully described for us by Isaiah 43: 7 in this manner: "Even every one that is called by my name; for I have created him for my glory, I have formed him; yea I have made him."

To accentuate this, let us read Job 10: 9: "Remember, I beseech thee, that thou hast made me as the clay; and wilt thou bring me into the dust again?"

Now let us get a broader view of this creature-man by reading Job 33: 4: "The spirit of God hath made me, and the breath of the Almighty hath given me life." Ah! here is a true evaluation of the dual natures of man.

The body can return to dust since it is clay. But the spirit, the other facet of the "breath of lives" (Gen. 2: 7) must return to God. Why? Because He gave it; it was part of Him—part of His being.

Man's destiny then was an eternal and immortal one. He was made to join the Lord's eternal sabbath from the works of the earth (Heb. 3: 7–18; Heb. 4) as he became translated (as was Enoch) to heaven in due course.

This the apostle Paul shows us in 1 Corinthians 15: 44: "It is sown a natural body, it is raised a spiritual body. There is a natural body, and there is a spiritual body."

This is something angels do not have. That is why the sinful angels are chained in the "tartarus" (2 Pet. 2: 4) awaiting their domicile of hell, prepared for them and the devil (Matt. 25: 41).

This proves, without a doubt, a dual nature of man—a natural body and a spiritual body. Because this is so, is why man, when he sinned, received the condemnation, "dying thou shalt die".

Like a beast, he now became just a "living soul", feeding his flesh and not his spirit—dying and decaying like a beast. That, in spite of the fact that man being of dual nature "does not live by bread alone but by every word that cometh out of the mouth of God". When he thus finally ceased on earth in the body, it is said of him in Ecclesiastes 12: 7: "Then shall the dust return to the earth as it was, and the spirit shall return unto God who gave it."

This process of dying, or of disintegration of the whole man, is described for us as follows in Genesis 6: 3: "My spirit shall not always strive with man, for that he *also* is flesh (not only spirit): yet his days shall be an hundred and twenty years."

Then in the seventh verse of Genesis 6 we read: "And the Lord said I will destroy man whom I have created from the face of the earth . . ."

Notice—since man is *also* flesh, the Lord projects to destroy him from the earth. But note—not in the spirit, since He here says in the seventh verse, He has created him (not formed him, as He had man's body).

WATCH THE DECAY

We read in Psalm 39: 11: "When thou with rebukes dost correct man for his iniquity, thou makest his beauty to consume away like a moth (spider): surely every man is vanity."

Something remains when man's body consumes away. Isaiah elucidates that for us in the tenth chapter, the eighteenth verse.

What remains of man? Ecclesiastes 12: 7 says "his spirit". Why? "Because God gave it from Himself."

Paul says in 1 Corinthians 15: 35–38 that man leaves just his body in the grave but remains a seed, or a soul.

Knowing this, faithful men are mindful that the devil has the "key of death" (Heb. 2: 14), but that the Lord has the issues of death . . . and as Revelation 1: 18 shows, "has the keys of (both) hell and death".

Such faithful men began to live after the spirit (Ezek. 18: 2–21), to live unto God because they knew that "God is a God of the living" (Luke 20: 37, 38). Thus, they believed as Moses put it in Genesis 15: 15: "And thou shalt go to thy fathers in peace; thou shalt be buried in a good old age." For such death brought peace, not the sabbath of God as yet (Heb. 3 and 4), but peace.

But to all others, whose "spirit was not made perfect" (Heb. 12: 23), "death has its sting" (1 Cor. 15: 56). That sting, of course, is sin, and one can feel it after the physical death in one's soul or in the spirit, because *it is the wage of sin*—or as we say in modern vernacular, the "pay off" (Rom. 6: 23).

Job 25: 6 describes man as follows: "How much less man, that is a worm? And the son of man, which is a worm?"

What part of man is a worm? His body? His soul? In Mark 9: 44 the Lord says: "Where their worm dieth not and the fire is not quenched."

The term *worm* here denotes the soul. It is so identified by *their* worm, or "their soul". It cannot be their body, for if you put a dead body into the grave, the body will decay. But a worm—put a worm into a grave and *it lives in the earth*!

What an apt similie for the soul, which is of God, and therefore cannot be held in a grave of dust. (Acts 2: 24–31; Ps. 16: 8.)

HOW TO HELP J.W.S

Now, how can we help Jehovah's Witnesses see this? No amount of argument would achieve this.

My textbook *Into the Light of Christianity* can become your textbook, Christian. With it you can undo the brainwashing that J.W.s have undergone and by its direction you can apply just the right modicum of the Word of God to heal their sick minds.

HERE IS HOW

Take two copies of *Into the Light of Christianity* along with you when you call upon the Jehovah's Witness.

Open your study with him with a prayer. First, read chapter 9, "Man Created in the Image and Likeness of God," page 115.

Read the first paragraph; ask questions; look up all scripture passages whether quoted or cited.

Continue with second paragraph. Duration for such a study should be no more than one hour.

Once chapter 9 is concluded, go on to chapter 10 which explains and debunks the J.W. doctrine: "Man is a Soul."

Then continue with chapter 11; "Immortality of the Soul Brought to Light by Jesus Christ."

Here the proper method is displayed for you. First you are establishing what Jesus, the prophets and apostles say about man. Then you crowd J.W.s by pinpointing what Jehovah's Witnesses say about man. In this manner you range Bible knowledge on this doctrine against Watchtower knowledge of this doctrine, and contrastively you demonstrate how more excellent is the Bible doctrine, since it was brought to light by none other than our Lord Jesus (2 Tim. 1: 10).

No other book, no other method, could debunk more effectively Jehovah's Witness brainwashing than does *Into the Light of Christianity* in your loving hands. Use it that way.

LESSON FIVE

How To Explain The Deity Of Jesus Christ

Jehovah's Witnesses say that (1) Christ was an angel in His pre-existence; (2) He was the man Jesus in His earthly existence; (3) He became a Spirit in His resurrection, not experiencing a bodily resurrection.

In this manner they have made the Lord as changing and changeable as is the entire human scene.

What we therefore have to show Jehovah's Witnesses from

Holy Writ is best described by Paul in Hebrews 13:8, that "Jesus Christ (is) the same yesterday, today and forever".

In John 1: 1–3, the apostle John introduces our Lord to the human scene as the Son of God.

The Lord's antecedents are clearly brought to view in the third verse of John 1, where we read: "All things were made by him; and without him was not anything made that was made."

As "who" did He make all things? Genesis 1: 1 answers: "In the beginning God created heaven and earth." It was as *the* God that He made all things.

Looking at this great truth from another side, or the human point of view, we see the premise raised by the apostle Paul in Colossians 1: 16, 17: "For by him were all things created, that are in heaven, and that are on the earth, visible and invisible, whether they be thrones, or dominions, or principalities, or powers: all things were created by him, and for him: and he is before all things, and by him all things consist."

Then, as the Creator of *all* things, who is He? Circumstantially, in the human view, comes this answer again from the apostle Paul. This time from Hebrews 3: 4 where we read: "For every house is builded by some man; but he that built *all* things is God."

Jehovah's Witnesses say that Christ "was the beginning of all creation; he was the first one created, an archangel."

Revelation 3: 14 says: ". . . These things saith the Amen, the faithful and true witness, the beginning of the creation of God."

Here is shown that the Lord Jesus began, or started, the Creation of God. Had he been the first one created, then this scripture would read, "The beginning of the creation *by* God."

As to Christ, and to His pre-existence, we read in Hebrews 1: 8: "But unto the Son he saith, thy throne, O God, is forever nd ever; . . . a sceptre of thy Kingdom!"

In Hebrews 7: 3 we receive further circumstantial proof where it is put in this manner: "Without father, without mother, without descent, having neither beginning of days, nor end of life; but made like unto the Son of God; abideth a priest continually forever."

Was the Lord Jesus then an archangel in His pre-existence

as Jehovah's Witnesses say? No. If Jehovah's Witnesses did not deny the doctrine of God—Father, Son and Holy Spirit—they would not get into this dilemma. For this doctrine reveals our God as *one God*; as Father, He created all things; as Son, He became the Redeemer; and as the Holy Spirit, He became the Sanctifier.

With the true doctrine of God in mind we read in Hebrews 1: 4, 5: "Being made so much better than the angels, as He hath by inheritance obtained a more excellent name than they. For unto which of the angels said He at any time, Thou art my Son, this day have I begotten thee? I will be to him a father and he shall be to me a son?"

Not only does the above quoted scripture passage show that the Lord is higher than any angel—yes, even an arch-angel—but it further brings to view His divinity. This becomes crystal clear by the above-made assertion that He is Heir of God.

This proves that not only was Jesus God the Creator in His pre-existence, but also that from His resurrection onward as the Son, He is now God—God, the Son, on the throne of God.

How fortunate for us that this is so; for, as Creator, the Father sits on the throne of judgment which condemns us all; and as Heir, or the Son, being our advocate with the Father on the judgment seat, He now sits on the right hand of the Father on the mercy seat.

Does this mean that Christ has usurped the throne of Jehovah, when we read in Hebrews 1: 6: "And again, when he bringeth in the first begotten into the world, he saith, and let all the angels worship him"?

If the Jehovah's Witnesses' *credo*, that our Lord Jesus was an archangel, is right, then this would proclaim to all the world the devil's contention, that the sovereignty of Jehovah had been usurped. In fact, by a quirk of reasoning, Jehovah's Witnesses do raise the question of sovereignty, in their nefarious doctrine of *Dualism*, that Jehovah is still God but must vindicate His sovereignty over Satan who is the god of this world in the Battle of Armageddon. But notice—all angels of God are commanded to worship Christ. As what? In a secondary worship? No. They are to worship Christ, God the Son Who is the Redeemer, *in primary worship*.

We have shown thus far, that Jehovah's Witnesses are wrong about the pre-existence of our Lord Jesus, and also have proven that they are wrong about His post-resurrection status. It remains for us now to show that they are also wrong about our Lord Jesus while He was the son of man.

In John 1 : 14, the Lord Jesus is introduced to us in the flesh as a man. In the same breath, however, He is also described for us in the eighteenth verse as "still *is* in the bosom of the Father", who is in heaven. He is at the same time in heaven as the Spirit, and on earth in the flesh.

As *who*? and as *what*? John introduces Him in the twenty-third verse, by quoting verbatim Isaiah 40: 3 (as the Jehovah's Witness's Bible shows) "as Jehovah".

Paul speaks of our Lord's coming into the flesh in this manner in Hebrews 2: 14: "Forasmuch then as the children are partakers of flesh and blood, he also himself likewise took part of the same, that through death he might destroy him that hath the power of death, that is, the devil."

Just how does this subjection of the Lord Jesus as God in the flesh look? Let us see. In Philippians 2: 6–9 we read this remarkable portrayal: "Who being in the form of God, thought it not robbery to be equal with God: but made himself of no reputation, and took upon himself the form of a servant, and was made in the likeness of men. And being found in fashion as a man, he humbled himself, and became obedient unto death, even the death of the cross. Wherefore God also hath highly exalted him, and given him a name which is above every name."

Here now began the subjection of the man Jesus which would eventually culminate into a subjection of all unto God again, and of all things which by His subjection He brought unto Himself (1 Cor. 25: 38; John 17: 3–5).

Our Lord played the man all right from the cradle to the grave. Dying as a man, He cried out, "Father why hast thou forsaken me?" As a sufferer He cried out in Gethsemane, "Father if it is thy will, let this cup pass from me." In honouring His Father in discussions He said, "The Father is greater than I." In speaking of divine purposes, He subordinated Himself as a man by saying, "It is not for *us* to know times and seasons."

Completely subjected to God as man, His deity nevertheless still shone through when He read the minds of men; when He forgave sins; when He was worshipped and served by both angels and men; when He stilled the raging sea; when He loved His enemies; when He healed the sick; when He raised the dead.

Only as God could He suffer. Only as God could He die. In doing so He swallowed up sin, condemnation and death—indeed, the sin of the whole world.

Not only that, but He eliminated the power of the devil, of death, and obtained for us the issues of life, "the keys of hell and death" (Rev. 1: 18). This He accomplished in being a partaker of flesh and blood (Heb. 2: 14).

I could not put it as well as the inspired apostle does in 2 Corinthians 5: 18, 19: "And all things are of God, who hath reconciled us to Himself by Jesus Christ, and hath given to us the ministry of reconciliation; to wit: *that God was in Christ*, reconciling the world unto himself in Jesus Christ . . ."

You see how easily can be debunked the Jehovah's Witness's statement that Jesus in His pre-existence was an angel; in His fleshly existence was a mere man; in His resurrection became a disembodied Spirit?

How can we help them see this? Obviously, a lot of time and effort has gone into brainwashing the Jehovah's Witnesses who stand before you. If you argue with them, you will only inflame their fanaticism to white-heat.

What can we do? Observe how a Jehovah's Witness becomes brainwashed.

He first buys a Watch Tower-published book. In backcalls the Jehovah's Witness excites him to read it. In a bookstudy at his home he is brainwashed. In another bookstudy in the Kingdom Hall he is indoctrinated. In still another study—the Watch Tower study in the Kingdom Hall—he is made theocratic-minded. In still another study he is trained to use these errors to brainwash you.

Bookstudies, then, is the road his indoctrination takes. That is his strong point. It is, however, also his weak point.

Instead of arguing, prevail upon him to have a bookstudy with you. Your textbook, especially written by a former Jehovah's Witness of long standing, who now has both kinds of knowledge, is *Into the Light of Christianity*. Train yourself in its effective use by following the above shown steps and directions. Follow them to the letter.

CHAPTER III

HOW TO WITNESS FOR CHRIST

(Acts 1: 8)

ALL the ages from John the Baptist backwards to Adam are filled with a hopeful looking for the "promised seed of the woman" (Gen. 3: 15). This looking for, this speculating about time, this chronologizing, had become second nature to all who lived within the dispensation of fragmentary gospels.

In His last instructions, "It is not for you to know the times and the seasons, which the Father hath put in His own power" (Acts 1: 7), the Lord put an end to all speculations about times and seasons. It is obvious to us, who study God's word, that all gospels of the past had the time element attached to them. They focused the eyes of all upon the coming of our Lord Jesus in the flesh into time. But these instructions of Acts 1: 7 plainly show that the end of the circle of Adam, offspring and time was now in sight for all who would believe in Jesus Christ.

Elsewhere the second Adam, our Lord Jesus Christ, is described as made a "quickening Spirit" (1 Cor. 15: 45). This "quickening" or life-infusing, our Lord had already demonstrated in this fashion in John 6: 63: "It is the spirit that quickeneth; the flesh profiteth nothing: the words that I speak unto you, they are spirit, and they are life." Faith in the Lord Jesus and in His words would become the "beginning of the new life in Christ". In this manner we would exit from out of time and flesh, sin and death, and enter into the circle of Jesus Christ, or reality.

How was the entering into this new life in Christ to be manifested?

HISTORIC DEMONSTRATION ON WITNESSING FOR CHRIST

The stage for the kick-off of witnessing for Christ is set for us in the statement of our Lord Jesus Christ in Acts 1: 8: "But ye shall receive power, after that the Holy Spirit is come upon you: and ye shall be witnesses unto Me both in Jerusalem and in all Judea, and in Samaria, and unto the uttermost parts of the earth."

Were they to become witnesses for Jehovah, as Israel had become after the Lord Jehovah rescued them from Egypt (Isa. 43: 10)? Such witnesses for Jehovah had talked about things of the past in the realm of "time". Such revelations had only come to few men: prophets, seers, kings, shepherds, a few women. Such witnessing, even in Moses, the foremost of them all, had been to point out "times and seasons" and the coming of the Lord Jesus Christ in the flesh. But here the Lord dismissed all "times and seasons" as having come to an end (Acts 1: 7). Now, He was telling them that "times and seasons" were solely in the power of the Father. Reality, the true universal, had come, and with it a new type of witnessing appeared.

This was not to be (and it is very important to get this context of Acts 1: 7, 8 clear in our minds at this stage) a witnessing about "times and seasons", about chronology or time speculations, about the past or the future. No. This was to be a witnessing as to what was now actually a life-like transformation taking place in the hearts of the witnesses. It was to display God's work in them, as the power of the Holy Spirit worked in and through them. These were to be the wellsprings of the "new life after the Spirit in Christ" (Prov. 20: 27).

This was dynamic, living, vibrant, present, spiritual, *The Work of God*! Whereas, the work of the Jews as Jehovah's Witnesses was about God and what He had done long ago outside of their persons, this witnessing for Christ was what God was actually doing right now in their hearts and lives.

Then came Pentecost. You read of it in Acts 2. Explaining this, Peter begins to elucidate this phenomenon in the 14th verse; then hark, as he heightens the action by making this remarkable statement: "But this is that which was spoken by the prophet Joel (Joel 2): and it shall come to pass in the last days, saith God, I will pour out my Spirit upon all flesh: and your sons and your daughters shall prophesy, and your young men shall see visions, and your old men shall dream dreams . . . and they shall prophesy." This was to have tremendous repercussions, graphically demonstrated for us in the 22nd verse:

"And it shall come to pass that whosoever shall call on the name of the Lord shall be saved . . ."

Filled with the Holy Spirit, Peter begins his remarkable testimony. This witness has ever remained the classic example of *"How to Witness for Christ"*. You read the details in Acts 2: 22–47. Christian witness, draw your instruction from there!

Rehearsing the deeds of the Lord in the past; retelling the stories of old; telling of the hope for the future; these were the themes for the Jews, the Jehovah's witnesses of history. Now, however, observe, the witness for Christ is a living, moving witness to a living Saviour, who resides right in the hearts of the witnesses. Who, then, is to participate in witnessing for Christ?

Just a few apostles, prophets, pastors, teachers and evangelists? This was to become a witnessing to life, extending a thrilling invitation to "whosoever will call on the name of the Lord". It was to become a witness of an entrance into a new circle of life; *life eternal after Jesus Christ.*

Upon sons, daughters, young men, old men, servants, handmaidens; upon every class, every sex, every age bracket; upon "whosoever will call upon the Lord"; would fall the unction for a new life in Christ.

This, therefore, would not be a witness to a word, a past act, a feat, a prophecy. This would be a witness of the Holy Spirit that a new life had begun in the heart of the witness. All of Acts shows *How to Witness for Christ*, how it began, how every Christian becomes involved, how whole congregations responded. Acts is a stupendous record of the *Witness for Christ.*

WHAT IS WITNESSING FOR CHRIST?

Speaking of the great sacrifice brought by our Lord Jesus Christ, Paul, in addressing himself to the sacrifice-conscious Hebrews (13: 13), draws this remarkable application, which depicts the *modus vivendi* of those "who are alive in Christ" by saying, "Let us go forth unto Him without the camp, bearing His reproach, for here we have no continuing city, but we seek one to come. By Him, therefore, let us offer the sacrifice of praise to God continually, that is, the fruit of our lips giving thanks to His Name . . ."

Three things would appear from the context of this discussion in Hebrews 13.

(1) Of what the Lord did for us and what He became to us.
(2) Of what the Lord expects us to do.
(3) Of what happens to others who hear us.

In three sub-headings I shall discuss this problem practicably.

WHAT THE LORD DID FOR US AND WHAT HE BECAME TO US

Our Lord Jesus Christ, who had created the human race (Gen. 1: 1; John 1: 1–3), came into our family of flesh by "partaking of flesh and blood" (Heb. 2: 14). When He came into our race He brought something very valuable with Him. He brought with Him the "righteousness of God" (1 Cor. 1: 30). But more than that, He also brought with Him the possibility of becoming a sacrifice for us, in His body, dying outside of the camp on the cross. Because He came to us as Saviour-God, He could emphatically say, "I am the Resurrection, and the Life, he who believes in Me . . . shall never die" (John 11: 25, 26), adding, in John 14: 6 "I am the Way, the Truth, and the Life."

In order to accomplish so great a salvation the Lord *came to us*. He reached out for us! Such grace was already promised us in Genesis 12: 3 and Isaiah 9: 6. With our Lord Jesus personified, came to us the "righteousness of God", since He, in person, is God. Coming to us in this manner was beautifully described for us by Paul in Romans 8: 32, "He who did not spare His own Son but gave Him up *for us all*, will He not also give us all things in Him?"

More, however, was involved in this *coming to us*. He came to us doing the will of His Father (John 6: 38) and in obedience became obedient to the Father in the flesh. Disobedience by Adam in the flesh, and subsequently by all of his progeny who followed him into flesh by birth, was the hall-mark of flesh. It had become a universal premise that obedience in the flesh must be the prerequisite for Him who would become our Saviour. Paul, therefore, says of the Lord Jesus appearing in flesh, "Though He were a Son, yet learned He obedience by the things which He suffered; and being made perfect, He became the Author of eternal salvation unto all them that obey Him (Heb. 5: 8, 9). This "will of the Father" *He did for us*, as an outreach! He desired it to be *ours*! He expresses this basic principle for life in Him, "I am among you as One who serves" (Luke 22: 27). In the 19th verse of this same chapter, He pinpointed this whole concept for us in this manner: "This is my Body, which is given for you."

How wonderfully this whole sacrifice has been projected for us in prophecy by Isaiah (43: 24), "You have burdened Me with your sins, you have wearied Me with your iniquities."

When He came to us, He came in the flesh, in the garb of a servant. Read of this fascinating entry, and of life from the cradle to the grave as a human, lived by the Son of God, in Philippians 2: 5-11. Appearing as Lord and servant, in mystic fusion of the divine and the human natures, Christ became to us and for us an actual demonstration of the act of "living in Christ". In this manner also, He brought the righteousness of God to us.

The entire concept of such a life in Christ, is in WITNESSING FOR CHRIST.

WHAT THE LORD EXPECTS US TO DO

It is said of our race that we were dead "in trespasses and sins" (Eph. 2: 1). Believing in our Lord Jesus Christ we "were forgiven our trespasses" (Col. 2: 13), and "All things are of God, who hath reconciled us to Himself, by Jesus Christ, and hath given to us the ministry of reconciliation, to wit: That *God was in Christ*, reconciling the world unto Himself, not imputing their trespasses unto them; and hath committed unto us the word of reconciliation" (2 Cor. 5: 18, 19).

In a nutshell, this scripture shows the enormity and magnitude of the extent of salvation which has come to us in Christ Jesus. He was *God in Christ Jesus* doing this marvellous work.

In the first place, all in the circle of Adam were dead. The context of 2 Corinthians 5, verse 14, shows that in this manner: "For the love of Christ constraineth us: because we thus judge, that if one died for all, then were all dead".

If we all were dead, then the dilemma of mankind is catastrophic! We cannot regard anything of value in the flesh in the face of this universal lot. Once we are saved and Christ begins to live in our heart, we can no longer regard anything in the light of the flesh. Our lot of having been snatched from the perdition prevailing in the old circle of Adam, has changed. How will this changed lot show?

Comes Paul and answers in 2 Corinthians 5: 15-17: "And that He died for all, that they which live should not henceforth live unto themselves, but unto Him which died for them, and rose again. Wherefore henceforth know we no man after the flesh: yea though we have known Christ after the flesh, yet now henceforth know we Him no more. Therefore if any man be in Christ, he is a new creature; old things are passed away; behold all things are become new."

What does Paul describe here? Paul answers, "new life". Just how is this new life articulated outwardly? Paul says in Romans 10: 10 that it is confessed (or breathed out) with the mouth. To this new creature, then, witnessing or confessing becomes as important as is breathing to the old creature. More so, it becomes a distinct kind of life by the very fervency of its zeal in witnessing as does a flower produce at the height of its metabolic processes in fragrancy. The Lord considered it thus, for do we not read in Heb. 13: 15 "By Him therefore let us offer the sacrifice of praise to God continually, that is, the fruit of our lips giving thanks to His name." The old creature after the flesh was enjoined in Leviticus to offer a praise offering too, but note what it is, "If he offer it for thanksgiving, then he shall offer the sacrifice of thanksgiving unleavened cakes mingled with oil, of fine flour, fried" (Lev. 7: 12). In Psalm 50: 14 this becomes more lucid where we read, "Offer unto God thanksgiving; and pay thou thy vows unto the most high."

Witnessing for Christ thus begins to take on the place of execution of vows and of thanksgiving offerings in mundane matters, using such things as moral obligations (Psalm 50: 14) and flour, cake, oil, as fleshly obligations and gifts. Owing to the "sacrifice of atonement" of our Lord's death for us, in faith accepting it, we owe, if we may call it that, "the sacrifice of thanksgiving", that is, witnessing for Christ. This becomes a demonstration of a gospel of power in our hearts. The whole power of the universe, and not just vows made, or cakes of oil, has been put behind this thanksgiving (Matt. 28: 18–20). In fact, this ministry of reconciliation (2 Cor. 5: 19) has been given us by our Lord Jesus Christ because we have experienced it ourselves, becoming because of this experience "authentic ambassadors for Christ".

Witnessing for Christ is a positive assertion of our faith. In its faithful daily performance it actually voices trust in God and in His salvation, articulating a new life (2 Cor. 5: 14–19). It vibrates in this manner confidence in the work of the Holy

Spirit under whose unction it operates (Acts 1: 8). In this context, witnessing suddenly appears as something more intrinsic than even our faith. What is more intrinsic than our faith in Jesus Christ? It is *trust* in Him, which really is an abiding faith "by which one endures to the end of one's life". He who witnesses for Christ with the aim of winning souls, demonstrates that his faith already is *life*, by inviting others to share Christ with him. This, by the way, is the same mode of giving, and of coming to us, in which the righteousness of God was brought to us by Jesus Christ.

We said "Witnessing for Christ is for the new creature what breathing is to the old creature after the flesh." If our new life in Christ is left inarticulate within ourselves it would remain life-less. Only in sharing this "living after the Spirit" with many, and observing this testimony bring new life into the hearts of others, as we spell out the language of the spirit, lies the reality of our life in Christ. As Christ comes to *live* (not sleep) in the hearts of others because they were excited by our report and followed through to receive the Lord Jesus in faith, we ourselves receive total assurance of our own salvation as we shall see later in the chapter: HOW TO WIN SOULS FOR CHRIST. It is alone, in this demonstration of faith to faith, that the "just shall live by faith". Is this the description of a silent layman? Or of an expert witness? Are you a layman, or are you a spiritual Christian?

Test yourself. What follows? If you have no personal testimony, no articulate expression of a faith which displays trust in Christ, ipso facto, you can receive no assurance that you have entered this new life in Christ, no more than would you live in the flesh if you stopped breathing. Because of this life-like aspect of such faith in Christ, we find many names, which are very descriptive, given to it. If you analyse these, they are really verbs of infinity. Perhaps already patterns for the universal life such as "life in Christ", or "Christ in us". Some others are "the work of the Lord", "confession", "power of God", "mercy", "truth", "righteousness". These all are in the final analysis "faith which is in Jesus Christ". They penetrate to a grasping of the well-springs of this new life. *They Encompass in Meaning* the new creation (2 Cor. 5: 17). Notice to what lengths and depths Paul carries this precept of the new life in Christ in Galatians 2: 20: It is no longer I who live, "but Christ liveth in me".

But where does this new life begin? Proverbs says, "The Spirit of man is the candle of the Lord . . ." It begins primarily by faith in the impression of "the image and likeness of God" upon the spiritual aspect of the soul of the Christian as he is born again "by water and the spirit" (John 3: 3–5). Thereafter, such new life is strengthened in growth in grace and truth as we shall see in the fourth chapter. Sweepingly, Paul describes this process for us all in a remarkable prayer recorded for us in Ephesians 3: 14–17: "I bow my knees unto the Father of our Lord Jesus Christ, of whom the whole family in heaven and earth is named, that He would grant you according to the riches of His glory *to be strengthened with might by His Spirit in the inner man*; that Christ may dwell in your hearts by faith . . ."

Born again, entertaining a "lively hope" (1 Pet. 1: 3), breathlessly in the flesh as we died with the Lord in baptism, we come alive after the similitude of His resurrection waiting upon the unction of power in which the commission to become a "witness for Christ" (Acts 1: 8) takes hold. As it does, the Holy Spirit begins to work out in us (Phil. 2: 12, 13) our salvation, or better, our escape from the flesh in a glorious deliverance of the Spirit over the flesh. A new life in Christ comes then out of the embryo of begetting of "water and the spirit" (John 3: 3–5) and a new creation begins to breathe by actual witnessing for Christ, and as it grows in grace and truth it becomes strengthened in evangelizing and soul winning. Finally it flowers into the full manhood or "the stature of the fullness of a man in Christ" (Eph. 4: 14).

The scriptural Christian, a new creation, reaches the stage of manhood in Christ only in growth in faith. As he does, he displays the "form of God" in the mode of life which is spiritual rather than mundane or fleshly, in the same way as the Lord did as recorded for us in Philippians 2: 5, 6. He subjects his flesh solely to bring into reality with his mouth and in his faith the "image of God" already being impressed in his inner man. He gives evidence of this growth by what he says with his lips. Once "witnessing for Christ" becomes our manner of life in the Spirit, then the new life in Christ is made the rule for this new life in our hearts. Our Lord becomes thus the new Strongman in our hearts. Firmly does that show in the witnessing from our lips (Rom. 12: 1; Heb. 13: 15, 16; Rev. 3: 20).

WHAT HAPPENS TO OTHERS WHO HEAR US

The prophet Isaiah in the sixtieth chapter, second verse, long ago described the lot of flesh as "darkness covers the earth, and gross darkness the people". In the stream of time, our Lord came as the light and began to shine in the land of darkness. He even said in John 8: 12: "He that followeth me shall not walk in darkness." Paul later shows that Christians are "not in darkness" (1 Thess. 5: 4). In spite of all this, John 3: 19 says, "Men loved darkness rather than light." Why this recalcitrance?

One outstanding reason for such obscurity is recorded for us in 2 Corinthians 4: 3: "But if our gospel be hid, it is hid to them that are lost: in whom the god of this world hath blinded the minds of them which believeth not, lest the light of the glorious gospel of Christ, *who is the image of God*, should shine unto them."

Failing to see in our Lord Jesus Christ the light, and the image of God, brings blindness to so many of our fellow men. This lack of spiritual perception beclouds salvation by faith. Faith in Jesus Christ brings to us the image of God. We read this best described for us in Romans 1: 16, 17: "For I am not ashamed of the gospel of Christ: for it is the power of God unto salvation to everyone that believeth; to the Jew first and also the Greek. For therein is the righteousness of God revealed from faith to faith: as it is written, The just shall live by faith."

Faith then is the power in the gospel of salvation, of Jesus Christ. It is faith that those who sit in darkness, however, lack. In this perspective, *Witnessing for Christ* looms large. Can you see it?

It pleases God, not through chronology, times and season prognostications (Acts 1: 7), *but through witnessing for Christ* (Acts 1: 8), by use of our lips and lives, by us who have experienced Christ, to condense the brilliance of salvation by God to things of the earth. Such things can be felt, touched and seen. Our witness must act like a condenser of that power of faith to levels usable by unenlightened ones. Our testimony of what the Lord Jesus means to us can effectively counteract the blindness regarding our Lord's coming as God and man. In faith (our faith) we can evoke by witnessing for Christ faith (in unbelievers) a demonstration of the reality of our new life in Christ.

The power lines of faith are strong in *Witnessing for Christ* (Acts 1 : 8). In fact, hereby evidence is given of the Holy Spirit at work in our hearts doing the work of God. This has dual repercussions.

On the one hand, it quickly establishes our faith (Acts 16: 5; Heb. 13: 9; Col. 2: 7; Rom. 16: 25); then, it demonstrates our faith as a "living faith" capable of transferring the boons of the new life in Christ unselfishly to others. Finally, it brings about an unusual subjection of our ego and a gradual merging of our new life in Christ.

On the other hand, this demonstration of a "living faith" via our witnessing for Christ, evokes faith in the hearts of others.

Incandescently lit now, by the Spirit of God (Prov. 20: 27), we truly can become persons who "let their light shine". In this role we remain steadfast in the place the Lord put us in and quietly sing forth the praises of thanksgiving unto our God for so great a salvation. Finally, by right associations, we are impelled to move on as a group into witnessing for Christ in an outreach. The "Let your light shine" aspect is often described as fishing with a pole for lost souls, one at a time. The "Go ye therefore" type is like "Casting out your nets", thus drawing in all kinds of fish. In subsequent visitation we again become stationary in the homes of such interested ones. Here, in an outreach of the personal contact, in a Bible study, we "let our light shine".

In these visitations we do not profess to have all the answers, nor are we afraid to admit this. When questions are äsked of us which we cannot answer, we are not dismayed. We simply tell them that we do not have the answer and promise to bring the answer back on our next visit. This will do two things: one, it will make us dig to find the answer; two, it will give our next visitation a purpose. Always remember, the fish you have caught in the net, or rather the people whom you are visiting, know less about Christ than you do. How do I know this? If they knew as much as you do, they would be out doing what you are doing.

In effective witnessing we turn the spotlights upon Jesus Christ. David had it right when he said in Psalm 31 : 1, "In thee, Lord, do I seek refuge; let me never be put to shame, in thy righteousness, deliver me." Note he says in "thy", not in "my" righteousness. This is the key-note of his testimony.

To be effective then your witness must, at first, be a testimony. You must witness as to how the righteousness of God became yours. Show them that it came to you by faith. Quote Romans 3: 28, where such acceptance is called "righteousness of God becomes ours", saying: "Thus is a man justified by faith."

How can you demonstrate to make it plausible to your hearer? Such faith has "the righteousness of God" which immediately swallows up sin, and that in a moment. The moment you believed in Jesus Christ as your Saviour, show, that in that moment you began to exist in Christ. By faith as yet, true; but you already can display the guarantee. You actually trust in this salvation, committing yourself wholly against that day, in which all mankind shall be judged, because you know in whom you have believed: Jesus Christ. You know that you have the righteousness as He, which is the Righteousness of God. That brings in peace and rest. Thus you have the prevenients: what the Lord did for you in faith, and the subsequents, of peace and joy in your heart, because of the first. That is your testimony and it is this which wins souls to Christ.

Let us bring this down to a very earthly view. Here is how I display it. For thirty years as a Watch Tower slave and a Jehovah's Witness, I grappled with the system of the NEW WORLD SOCIETY trying to maintain a righteousness which would save me in Armageddon. There was in this, nothing new; nothing that other condemned humans in other strata of society did not experience. But that morning on April 18, 1952, when in faith I believed in Jesus Christ, at once the righteousness of God came to me, and swallowed up all my sins and from that moment on I have fully trusted, and still fully trust, that He is my righteousness. *That one fact made my life entirely new*, in every way.

Note, the testimony is crystal clear. It raises up Jesus Christ as the Saviour who for me turned my life from a "life in trespasses and sins" and brought in "a new life in Christ", with peace and joy. This demonstrates that faith is the power unto salvation. The dealing of the Lord with my heart that night, when all my works were knocked out, was the condenser. Your witness for Christ, can lead to repentance in your hearer, when he is brought to accept the Lord as Saviour, urged on by you in your testimony of how it worked for you, and your quotes of salvation Scripture texts.

COMING THE WRONG WAY UNTO SALVATION

Since it is so important to come the right way unto salvation, it is not surprising that the devil would invent many wrong ways. There is only one way (John 14: 6), and that is through our Lord Jesus Christ. Since men often are prone to "wrestle scriptures to their own destruction", which pattern is evolved for them by the very devil himself who often quotes scriptures out of context (Matt. 4: 6–9; Luke 4: 10), there can be only one, unchanging, valid way, our Lord Jesus Christ; of whom it is said, "Jesus Christ the same yesterday, today and forever" (Heb. 13: 8).

In what way does a new creature from its spirit-begetting in faith travel out of the embryo to a breathing life in Christ when it is born again, on to maturity and beyond? By emulating the example our Lord Jesus set while on earth, from the Jordan to the cross. Of our Lord it is said that He "is the faithful and true witness". He sets in this manner the norm for us, or the way to travel. By becoming "faithful and true witnesses" for Christ, in which there are no "ifs" and "buts", we can lead souls to Christ. The testimony, the witness of what the Lord Jesus did for you, *is* the best way to win souls for Christ, if you back it up with salvation texts of the Bible.

Men devise ways. In my book *Thirty Years a Watch Tower Slave*, you read of how my family at the end of World War I were driven from their homestead. Losing everything, they were dumped into the big city of Berlin. There they were trying to readjust themselves and their lives.

In the world at that time the way of the Watch Tower Society was at work. It fastened its hold upon the historical problems of the times, misusing the Bible for that end. Not heeding the Lord's warning in Acts 1: 7, it began to dabble in "times and seasons", in chronology and time prophecies. The Society came and told us that in its books we could learn how we could be saved in these last days on earth.

Notice how error works? If you give your testimony of what Christ means to you by witnessing, you will back that up with salvation Scriptures. If you follow Satan's way of "times, seasons and chronology" you will tear scripture out of context to speculate. This way you will lead others astray, as you have been led astray by the devil. That is called "wrestling scripture to your own destruction".

This organization averred that the books offered furnished new light, better light than men had ever had. Foolishly, we bought and read the books, forgetting that the devil always offers new light, better light; forgetting that already in the garden of Eden the devil had offered better knowledge than God had given men.

As Lutherans we had been thoroughly indoctrinated in the Word of God and we had a healthy respect for the Word of God. But never before had we seen such a juggling act of God's Word, and we mistook that for better description and handling of God's Word, and became beguiled. The only way this method of the devil can be combated is, to *Witness for Christ*.

It did not bring Christ. It talked a lot about Christ. In fact, in those years Russellism was a half-and-half affair. This made us forget that when our Lord Jesus appeared on earth, *He had become the Light*, unchanging everlastingly effective to dispel arkness.

In reading these books my mind soon became far more concerned with such scriptures used by the Watch Tower in an odd way to demonstrate that in 1925 Abraham, Isaac and Jacob would return to this earth as princes and that "millions now living would never die". I became so imbued with that slogan I sold thousands of copies of the booklet with this title.

When 1925 came and Abraham, Isaac and Jacob did not show, I was disappointed. But clever explanations by Judge Rutherford, who one night addressed us at headquarters in Magdeburg, Germany, in May 1925, assuaged my misgivings. He told us that night among other things, "Boys, you do not want to go to heaven now when the Lord has so much work for us to do. Let us print books and go with them into the highways and byways and: advertise, advertise, advertise, the King and kingdom until the end shall come." He talked two hours that night and when he was through, he had talked us foolish ones out of going to heaven.

From that time on, I for one, became obsessed with the idea of establishing the Kingdom on earth in the flesh. As time wore on, we who were young, were thoroughly trained in the way of the Watch Tower, and soon thousands became imbued with the same spleen. This way became so right in my eyes, that I would have died for it. I was arrested sixteen times, mobbed twice, stoned once. I carry to this day a hole in my head, which resulted from being almost brained in the break-up of a lecture in Germany, where I was the speaker.

This way, which seemed so right to me, had nothing about Christ in it. The witnessing work done by me as a Jehovah's Witness did not raise up Christ as my Saviour, nor about what He had done for me. My witness in those days was what the NEW WORLD SOCIETY meant to me and what it would do for you, if you would come in with us. I would tell you: "If you listen and become one of Jehovah's Witnesses, you shall be saved in Armageddon. If you do not hear me, you shall be destroyed in Armageddon." Jesus Christ, you see, was never raised up!

What an awakening I had in the morning of April 18, 1952! My works, all shattered about me, brought me low to despair. It was then I saw Jesus Christ as my Saviour. What a difference that made that morning. The Heavenly Father heard my desperate prayer once I forgot about my foolish works as a Jehovah's Witness, and by His grace sent faith into my heart. Thus He led me to Jesus and by faith all sins were forgiven, and a new life began in peace and joy. That is MY TESTIMONY, to which quickly was added the Word of God. This testimony and Word I have used before audiences aggregating some 665,000 persons in some 48 different denominations; and in my three books. Once I took pride in the fact that I had baptized 463 new converts into the Watch Tower movement. Since I have become a witness for Christ, the Lord has USED my testimony about Him, what He became to me, to bring 7,918 Jehovah's Witnesses to Christ that I know of, in four short years. Can you see the power of faith operating in the *Witness for Christ*, because it is *reality*?

RAISE UP CHRIST

Jehovah's Witnesses still preach, dealing in many words, by the printed page of their books. But "the kingdom of God comes not by words, but by power" (1 Cor. 4: 20). Millions of books published by Jehovah's Witnesses cannot save a soul. But the testimony of what the Lord Jesus means to you, if you are saved, and backed up by the Word of God and its promises, can *save*! Witnessing for Christ, therefore, is not accomplished by the printed page, even such Life Messengers are printed in the nicest fashion, or have the finest colours as displayed in Watch Tower books, nor by words, nor even by might, *but by my Spirit* (Acts 1:8). That is so decreed by the Lord.

Let me here insert. I do not disparage the value of the printed page. On the contrary, I hope and pray historic Christianity becomes as adept in using it as today are the Jehovah's Witnesses. The printed page is only, however, advertising Christ in the first stage reaching men in circumstances when no witness for Christ is around, as, for instance, it did for the eunuch reading Isaiah. Notice though, it took Philip to lead him to Christ, the Life Messenger printed in Isaiah couldn't do it.

Witnessing for Christ, from the lips of a saved one, however, is better. It is a living testimony of what the Lord Jesus Christ becomes to *us*. Through our souls and body, in wonderful by-play of demonstrating this new life in Christ, the Holy Spirit begins to write in our hearts of flesh the "image of God". Just think of it! What power looms up here! Are you poised as were the disciples before Pentecost, to receive it? All, comes by faith.

In this unique manner we are prepared by the Holy Spirit to become an epistle for Christ, or an individual chapter. This is not done with paper and ink, nor with a chisel on a tablet of stone, but by the Holy Spirit in the tables of our fleshly hearts.

Thus the witness of a Christian, his testimony and the quotation of the Word of God to back up the invitation, is the best evangelizing and soul-winning book ever written and becomes a true life-like Life Messenger, and not just a book or booklet in print.

PRACTICAL SUGGESTIONS FOR WITNESSING

The greatest part of promotion of the gospel of Jesus Christ is motion. That is why our commission in Matthew 28:19, 20, starts out "Go ye therefore . . ." Paul shows that "feet that move to bring tidings of peace" are beautiful, and in this he quotes from Isaiah 52:7 where we read: "How beautiful upon the mountains are the feet of him that bringeth good tidings, that publisheth peace; that bringeth good tidings of good, that publisheth salvation; that said unto Zion, Thy God reigneth."

Jehovah's Witnesses have been sold the idea of a subverted gospel by use of the printed page or published Life Messengers. To keep them busy the Watch Tower fastened onto these texts and truths. It established early in 1925 the position of a Kingdom Publisher (1926 Watch Tower, Covenantor Sacrifice which?), and has made Jehovah's Witnesses the legmen of a super sales organization for its books, booklets and magazines. To create levers for control it exacts a rigid time counting and reporting set-up. This is done for two reasons. 1. To keep Jehovah's Witnesses busy so they do not realize that they are not saved and do not have a new life in Christ, which alone counts. 2. To build up by their activities a NEW WORLD SOCIETY. Jehovah's Witnesses have become very good at this type of witnessing.

But what about us, who have Christ, who really should be "life" messengers? There are two kinds of witnessing across our paths who are in and have Christ. First "Let your light shine" type of witnessing. The other, the "Go ye therefore" type. We will concern ourselves in this discussion, with the "Let your light shine" type of witnessing. The other, the "Go ye therefore . . ." type will be discussed in chapter 7: HOW TO ORGANIZE GROUP WITNESSING.

All of us live in a neighbourhood and in any populous country people are everywhere. These people have in common with us the same type of body. But most of them do not have in common with us "this new life in Christ". What an opportunity and what a challenge!

People move about frequently. Often, upon coming into a new community, they fail to immediately find a church home. There they sit, easy prey for Jehovah's Witnesses and other cultists, who cover such territories every six weeks.

Here is where the *Witness for Christ* should constantly operate. The primary aspect of witnessing for Christ, amidst such changing groups of people in our neighbourhood and amidst our acquaintances, is that of advertising this "new life in Christ" by letting your light shine.

Jehovah's Witnesses are taught, that in 1919 to 1922, the Lord revealed to them the use of the printed page as LIFE MESSENGERS, to "Advertise, Advertise, Advertise, the King and the kingdom". The Watch Tower Society handed Jehovah's

Witnesses multi-coloured books containing a false gospel. Since these were LIFE MESSENGERS without a personal testimony, such as a *Witness for Christ* alone could give, they brought error to those who bought them.

These books do not witness, but really render judgments from the temple upon various classes of humans and that when people buy them at their doors it marks such as "other sheep" to be won for the THEOCRACY.

Since then, by persistent promotion which was almost all motion from door to door, they have subverted and converted 1,100,000 baptized Kingdom Publishers and are presently indoctrinating some 10,000,000 people in the world in some 168 lands, who are being processed in various stages of subversion. Think, what would happen if all Christians became LIFE MESSENGERS, and began daily to advertise "this new life in Christ" which, as we have shown in this chapter, is not a dream, but the reality of eternal life. Witness for Christ and the new life in Him, *is* advertising Christ! Let us not leave it to the printed page, let us ourselves, witness with the living Word.

Do you understand that now? All right, now for some examples. Get to know your immediate neighbours. If you cannot do it in a conversational way, why not do something nice for them. If you are a housewife, make some of your best cookies and bring a batch of these over to your neighbour some day and in a friendly manner start a conversation. In the course of the conversation find out whether or not they are churched. Find out whether they are Christians. Many churched people are not, you know. Then tell them about your church and when and where you go. If they are unchurched invite them, if churched, chum with them. By doing this, you will have put your light in a position to shine: for from that moment on you will be watched by them. Display Christ and your new life in Him by actually living it before them. What an opportunity!

If you have tradesmen coming regularly to your home, set up your lamp. Give tone to all your future conversations by witnessing for Christ at the very outset. Be a good and friendly customer and let your light shine by witnessing for Christ, every time. You will be amazed how many of these tradesmen can be won for Christ. Witnessing for Christ, in a hundred and one such aspects is the harbinger of your progress.

The moment you build a wall around yourself, and your church, you will put your light under the bushel. Being of the church, the light of the church will shine. But your individual light will be out, hiding under the bushel of the church. The moment your individual light stops shining, that moment will also see the beginning of your loss of identity in the universal church. Then your own spiritual progress will slow down and eventually come to a full stop. All the time you may still be a member in good standing in your church.

Progress in growth in grace and truth stops the moment a Christian stops asserting his identity as an individual in Christ as a witness. Once His measure, given unto each of us individually (Eph. 4: 7), stops performing in witnessing and visitations, from that moment your need to dig in God's Word to keep abreast ceases, because you no longer have need for it. Soon, you will have stopped reading God's Word daily. Not too long afterwards you will have become frustrated and as you continue hearing the Word of God every Sunday in this condition, it will prick you, gradually dull you, finally kill you. You will have become hardened in unbelief.

The way to defeat the devil's efforts to thus kill your new life in Christ, and also to blind our fellowmen around about us to so great a salvation which we have in Jesus Christ, *is by our constant, earnest, sincere, enthusiastic presentation of the truth of the new life in Christ.* Advertise, Advertise, Advertise Jesus Christ as your living Saviour by witnessing for Him in letting your light shine, then you will be truly a LIFE MESSENGER.

But other aspects are intertwined here. Four basic things come to our minds when we think of the manner of witnessing for Christ. This goes for both aspects, the "Let your light shine" and the "Go ye therefore . . ." type.

(1) Our witness must be an expression of our faith in our own salvation.

(2) Our witness must give evidence, in the way it is being rendered, that we are sent. Actually by calling, experience and testimony we are ambassadors for Christ. It must be outside of the camp, in our neighbourhood, in the highways and the by-ways, at work and in public. It is most effective when conducted in a group style like the proverbial casting of a net, in a systematic working of a territory from house to house.

Witnessing is not to sell books, or to distribute printed

matter solely, but to present Christ. Look at the example set in Acts 2: 46, 47.

It should be done with thanksgiving and prayer. It must, at all times, be an outreach outside of the church and a sharing with others with whom we have a body of flesh in common.

(3) Our witness must be spoken by us as a communication, in a personal contact, so that it can be heard as a personal message.

(4) Our witness for Christ must be presented as a testimony of what Christ has done for us, describing how our burden, which we carry from the past to the present, has been made light by the Lord. No longer under the actual slavery of sin and death, freed by the Lord Jesus as we are from these scourges by faith, we now witness about freedom in Christ. The same burden as that of the past, but how much lighter by faith?

Thus you see there is no more general way in which lost souls may be helped to see Christ than by way of witnessing for Christ. That is true in "letting your light shine" and in "Go ye therefore . . ." (Matt. 28: 19, 20).

"Cast your bread upon the waters and after many days it will return", is nowhere more true than in witnessing for Christ. Repeat again and again, the old, old story of Jesus and His love, always remembering how long it took us to hear it and believe it. I, for one, shall never grow weary of repeating it, for it took me thirty-one years to hear. Make it simple, but tell it often, put it across with real enthusiasm.

But more important to ourselves, witnessing is the way "we present our bodies a holy, living sacrifice, which is our reasonable service" (Rom. 12: 1). In this manner we live by faith in Jesus Christ.

Every time we tell a fellow human being about our Lord Jesus Christ and what He has done for us, we are not only giving a positive expression of our faith, but we are advertising Him. The oftener this is done, the surer we ourselves will become of our salvation which will tend to stabilize us in living after the Spirit. In this way we take our stand and become a witness "letting our light shine" to advertise Jesus Christ as our Saviour. How needful this is, with so many false ways promulgated in the world.

More than that appears. By witnessing we give evidence that we have not grasped salvation to keep it for ourselves only, to hoard it in our hearts, but we are afforded the opportunity to keep our faith alive, vibrant, growing. Otherwise we would become dead Christians with a built-in rigidity, and the spiritual death of rigid rituals and ceremonies or worship would engulf us. Our lips, present a "living Saviour" who lives within our hearts if we witness for Christ. This we prove by constantly talking about Him to others. The mouth overflows with that which has filled the heart.

Every Christian, or Christ-like one, is also a sheep. When Adam and Eve were joined together in holy wedlock, they were blessed "to multiply and replenish the earth". As we become Christ's bride, joined with Him in one spirit, we, too, must give evidence of the blessedness of this new life in Christ. We must increase it by multiplying it.

Always remember that sheep always beget sheep in increase; not the shepherd. Our Lord graciously gives us gifts in our pastors, teachers and evangelists. Their job is, as we read in Ephesians 4: 12, "the perfecting of the saints, the work of the ministry, the edifying of the body of Christ".

As sheep, our job is to bring increase into the house of God and hand it over to them so that they can perform their labour of love for which they were set aside by divine ordinance.

But like they, we, who are not pastors, teachers and evangelists, have received gifts too, as shown in Ephesians 4: 7, a measure of the Spirit, our measure or identity in Christ, and together the sheep and the shepherd form a team, dedicated to reach maturity in Christ (Eph. 4: 14).

They preach sermons, the Word; we witness what the Lord Jesus means to us, drawing sheep into the fold, for the shepherds to tend. We are a team of equals or men in Christ.

How long shall this be? "Till we all come into the unity of the faith and the knowledge of the Son of God, and a perfect man, unto the measure of the fulness of Christ."

When these new ones are trained, they too must go out and say, "Come" (Rev. 22: 17).

CHAPTER IV

HOW TO EVANGELIZE FOR CHRIST OR MAKE THE PERSONAL CONTACT

(Prov. 27: 17)

WHAT CONSTITUTES AN EVANGELIST?

As we look upon the synoptic gospels of Matthew, Mark and Luke, we see in them a presentation of Jesus Christ the man, by men who truly were evangelists. In the compilation of reports their literary personalities amounted to nothing. What they wrote about was already common knowledge in the Christian community. These traditions were reduced to writing by these men exactly as they were current. Because these men presented the life of Jesus Christ as the early Christian community had experienced it, without developing their own narratives around it, is why they are properly called evangelists.

Evangelizing is therefore a word which has the term "angel" in its middle. "Angel" means "messenger." A messenger is one who carries a message as he receives it with the intent of conveying it exactly as he received it, without adding anything of his own to it. He himself does not enter into it. A true evangelist, therefore, will never argue his own views, but present Jesus Christ to the lost. He knows that the moment he indulges in anything of his own in arguments, etc., that that moment he will fail to be an evangelist. For the moment he argues, the mind of his listener closes to what he says, as the listener begins to formulate in his mind a reply to the argument. To communicate or evangelize Christ is a personal follow-up of a witness for Christ to a lost soul, and is exacting work, demanding able workmanship on a par with that of Matthew, Mark and Luke.

EVANGELIZING IN ACTION IN THE FIRST CHURCH

With the opening demonstration of the power of witnessing for Christ behind it, the Church began to employ the word of God and the witness of the Holy Spirit, to excite men to come unto Jesus Christ. In Acts 2: 41–42 we read, "Then they that gladly received his word were baptized; and the same day there were added unto them about three thousand."

The huge success of this initial witness for Christ, however, did not becloud the need for a continuous use of God's Word and a study therein. Note, we continue reading in verse 42, "And they continued steadfastly in the apostles' doctrines and fellowship, and in breaking of bread, and in prayers."

This kind of witnessing, backed by studying and prayer, is described as a continuing action, spilling over from the temple to a perambulating ministry from house to house. "And they, continuing daily with one accord in the temple, and breaking bread from house to house, did eat their meat with gladness and singleness of heart" (verse 46). Note, it is from this procedure that we culled out what in Chapter VI is called the TRAINING, TEACHING AND TELLING PLAN, and it is from this procedure here, from which we got the idea of a MID-WEEK WITNESSING, STUDYING AND PRAYER MEETING of two-and-a-half-hour duration.

With a continuing witnessing programme, it became necessary for the early Christian to be well versed in the use of the Scripture in order to communicate Christ. Ignorance is in this realm everywhere censured, on the basis of practicability. Peter says, "Be ready always to give an answer to everyone who asketh us a reason for the hope that is in us." Jude says, "Earnestly contend for the faith which was once delivered to the saints." You see that ignorance at once branded such a person as not being "in Christ".

Note how studiousness in God's Word is praised. The Bereans are commended for their type of careful study of God's Word (Acts 17: 10–12). The whole Church is admonished to "study to show themselves approved" (2 Tim. 2: 15). These are only a few instances in which personal study is commended.

Ecclesiastes 12: 12 shows that "much studying is a weariness of the flesh", and if one still lives in the flesh, then it will be almost impossible for such an one to study to show himself approved after the Spirit. Only if one is in Christ, living after the Spirit, and has advanced from witnessing for Christ to evangelizing or communicating Christ to others, will this weariness of the flesh for studying be overcome. For then, as an evangelist, will the Christian have become a messenger, and himself, his flesh, will have been impressed into the service of the Lord.

IMPRESSIVE EXAMPLES OF PERSONAL EVANGELISM

It is not surprising, therefore, that we discover in the early Church everywhere marvellous examples of personal evangelism. To our minds at once leaps the extraordinary experience of Philip. He was one of the seven laymen selected by the apostles to wait on the tables (Acts 6: 5). He was not of the brethren dealing with the Word of the ministry, the clergy. Faithfully Philip carried out his duties in Jerusalem. Then came the day when Saul persecuted the Church and scattered them abroad from Jerusalem. Such excellent witnesses were *all* these Christians that everyone went preaching everywhere. Philip went to Samaria. He went there and preached Christ, and also became a soul winner in the sense in which we shall discuss soul winning in Chapter IV. Then he brought many to believe in Christ, and baptized them. This marvellous success of witnessing and evangelizing by the layman Philip brought the apostles to Samaria. Philip immediately turned over these sheep to the Ministers of God, and they laid on the hand of fellowship, and the Holy Spirit came upon them. Read this remarkable story in Acts 8: 1–25.

With the work done in Samaria, the Lord asked Philip to go south. On his way there, this happened to this remarkable layman: "And he arose and went: and behold, a man of Ethiopia, an eunuch of great authority under Candace, Queen of the Ethiopians, who had charge of all her treasure, and had come to Jerusalem for worship, was returning, and was sitting in his chariot reading Esaias the prophet. Then the Spirit said unto Philip, Go near, and join thyself to this chariot. And Philip ran thither to him, and heard him read the prophet Esaias, and said, Understandest thou what thou readest? And he said, How can I, except some man should guide me? And he desired Philip that he would come and sit with him."

Here is a marvellous portrayal of true communicating of Christ. First, Philip is sent, and makes thus the first move. Had he stayed at home in Jerusalem he would never have come into this marvellous situation where the Holy Spirit could use him. Second, having gone forth, or made the first move, he comes upon a man in need. This man already believed in God. Now he wanted understanding. Philip began at once to evangelize, by studying God's Word with the eunuch Ethiopian. But most important of all, note how competent Philip had become since the day he had been selected a deacon to wait upon tables at Jerusalem, in being a witness and an evangelizer for Christ. He led, by his faith, his zeal, and his competence in the use of the Word of God, the Ethiopian to Christ.

Another important aspect of Philip's life is recorded for us in Acts 21: 8, 9, "And the next day we that were of Paul's company departed and came unto Caesarea: and we entered into the house of Philip the evangelist, which was one of the seven: and abode with him. And the same man had four daughters, virgins, which did prophesy." Not only had Philip who started to wait on tables in Jerusalem become an evangelizer, but note, all of his four daughters were doing the same work. In fact, all true Christians in those days were witnesses, evangelizers and soul winners!

Another example was Stephen, also one of those seven deacons or laymen. His testimony became so effective that he was found worthy to seal his testimony with his life. The first martyr for Christianity, note, was not an apostle, or a pastor, or teacher, HE WAS A LAYMAN—a layman who had become an expert witness for Christ.

Witnessing, evangelizing and soul winning, therefore, was the ideal. It made for increase in numbers, but also increase in growth of grace and truth in those participating in it. Such remained steadfast in the doctrines of the apostles. This "new life in Christ", or the righteousness of God in them, *came to them* (Rev. 3: 20), when the Lord Jesus entered their hearts, and did not come to them by the performance of special works, rites, contemplations, mediations; and all that their souls could do did not help. This "new life in Christ" came to them *only by faith*, and was *sustained by the Word of God*. "Man shall not live by bread alone, but by every word that proceedeth out of the mouth of God" (Matt. 4: 4).

As we look upon witnessing, evangelizing, all across the board in the early Christian Church, something becomes quite obvious. The "new life in Christ" cannot flourish except it has the Word of God to feed on daily. Where the Word of God is missing, there is no help for this "new life in Christ". It will die still-born. If we have the Word of God, we are rich and lacking nothing, since in us, who "are alive in Christ", the Word of God becomes, *ipso facto*, liberty, wisdom, power and every blessing. This is why the entire 119th Psalm, in David's pungent words, yearns for the hearing of the Word of God.

We see, then, that to "those who are alive in Christ", and are born again of water and the Spirit (John 3: 5), there is no more terrible disaster with which we can be afflicted than a famine of the hearing of the Word of God (Amos 8: 11). This famine, this great affliction, is very evident today in Christianity. Back in the days of the apostles, even while they were still alive on the scene, it began to spread across the scene. It had, then, tremendous repercussions. I will discuss a few of these shortly. But to us, who face this famine in Christianity today, may I say, Let us all pray in Christianity fervently, and work for mercy, believing the facts reported for us in Psalm 107: 20: "He sent his word and healed them, and delivered them from their destructions."

Christ was sent into the world to minister to that Word. Moreover, the entire segment of gifts for Christianity (Eph. 4: 8–14), all apostles, prophets, pastors, evangelists and teachers, have been called out, and have become instituted BUT FOR ONE PURPOSE: *for the ministry of the Word of God.* That is how important the Word of God is!

If in our Christian congregations today, with their blessed autonomy "of hiring their preachers" still intact, there are pastors, teachers and evangelists who do not preach the Word, then let the congregations dismiss them and get a faithful man into the pulpit who PREACHES THE WORD (2 Tim. 4: 2).

In looking upon early Christianity we find that she displayed the arts of witnessing, evangelizing and soul winning for Christ, because *faith and the Word of God rule the "new life in Christ"* which she lived. Christianity: AWAKE!

ANTI-CHRIST CONCEPT OF ANOTHER GOSPEL

The gospel of Jesus Christ, if believed, brings in a "new life in Christ", and allows in performance of the fundamentals of witnessing, evangelizing and soul winning, the new life to *breathe* and *live*.

How did it come into being? By Christ entering into the heart of the believer (Rev. 3: 20). It expresses itself in witnessing for Christ (Acts 1: 8), because it articulates in this manner the Holy Spirit.

We have noted elsewhere that other gospels had been predicated upon preaching "times and seasons" (Acts 1: 7). This concept is called a false gospel (Gal. 1: 6–9). In practice, it appeared early. Paul had to chastise the Thessalonians who predicted definite dates for the Lord's return. In the fifth chapter of first Thessalonians Paul culminates his entire argument against "times and seasons" by saying, "But of the times and the seasons, brethren, ye have no need that I write unto you" (v. 1). Why? Because they really knew that these things were in the hands of the Father (Acts 1: 7).

It is here that we can put the finger upon the true beginnings of heresy in our midst. The true gospel shows Christ to be our salvation. Its preaching is our "new way of life". The false gospel is to preach what others will do in due time, or do for you, if you do what they want you to do.

In order for this false gospel to succeed it had to attack the deity of our Lord Jesus Christ, for in denying the deity of Christ it is impossible to have Christ enter into one's heart.

Many "false prophets" already had gone out into the world in John's day (1 John 4: 1). But it remained for a man called Cerinthus to formulate this attack. Irenaeus, in his *Against Heresies*, Bk. 1, ch. 26, tells us what Cerinthus taught: "He portrayed Jesus as not being born of a virgin, but as the son of Joseph and Mary, born in the ordinary way. . . . After his baptism Christ descended upon him in the form of a dove from the Supreme Potentate and performed miracles. But at the end Christ left Jesus. Then Jesus suffered and rose again, while Christ, as a spiritual being, remained incapable of suffering."

Since this false gospel was an attack upon a living Christianity, it had to be carried abroad from house to house. Since perambulating was a common practice in all Christian circles in those days, heretics began to travel, too. Yes, they used the same methods Christians did. Paul warns of such who go into the homes of people for Bible studies, with the intent to subvert (2 Tim. 2: 26; 3: 6).

Nothing is more effective than house-to-house work by all concerned, which is followed up in return calls. It is not surprising, therefore, that these false doctrines culminated in the Arian heresy, which even succeeded in subverting the Christian Church for a while. Gnostics, Manicheans, Montanists, Pelagians, and many others attacked successfully the Christian Church in its universality or catholicity, and riddled it with heresy. In this way the spiritual balance of the Church, its universality in Christ on the one hand, and the identity of the individual in his relationship with Christ on the other hand, was destroyed for a while by such tactics.

Thanks to the valiant stand by the Church, the Arian heresy was beaten down, and the doctrine of Christ upheld, restoring the universality of the Church. However, mistaking the witnessing by all laymen, as their measure of the Spirit (Eph. 4: 7) to the faith that was in them, as the cause for the rise of heresy in its attack upon the universality of the Church, the Church forbade this outlet. Unfortunately this led to a curtailment in the study of the Word of God by the so-called laymen, since, after all, "much study is a weariness to the flesh." If you are not using the Word of God to go and evangelize, why soon its need vanishes.

The Reformation committed the same error later, clamping personal witnessing, evangelizing and soul winning under the bushel of "Ecclesiasticism".

With new freedom in reformed circles, it was impossible for long to hold down the forces of heresy, who first appeared in the form of Anabaptists, later Seventh Day Adventists, Christian Scientists, Mormons and Jehovah's Witnesses.

Christianity has lost sight of the true fundamentals of its faith. AWAKE, Christians, it is almost too late! Not only are these fundamentals, the "doctrines once delivered to the saints", but also included are the arts of witnessing, evangelizing and soul winning. The former uphold the universality or catholicity of the Church, and the latter express the identity of each convert in it, according to its measure of the Spirit (Eph. 4: 7). This is the agency for life in Christianity.

Without its practice today, and that on the broadest scale,

there looms up an imbalanced Christianity, engulfed in cults on one side and sects on the other: cults in expressing identity, sects in expressing an attack on universality. Most Christians today are asleep, and because of that have remained "babes in Christ". In my travels throughout Christendom, in forty-eight denominations to be exact, I have found that faithful pastors find it entirely impossible to organize personal evangelizing and witnessing. Most Christians termed "laymen" are incapable of giving an intelligent account of their faith.

When I was Zone servant in the NEW WORLD SOCIETY I instructed thousands of Kingdom Publishers on how to deal with Christians. We used to say: "The religionist cannot defend his faith. Attack it. Make him smart in his inability to defend it. RUB IT IN. Then, when you have done that, put the onus on the clergy and upon their work, showing the laymen that their ignorance is due to the system built up and controlled by the clergy." Like the Nicolaitans of old, condemned by the Lord and the Church (Rev. 2: 6, 15), in this manner we made the clergy the whipping boy. By superior fast-talking arguments we would draw thousands of Christians who had unfortunately never grown to manhood, but who had stayed retarded "babes in Christ" too long, into our system. Then we would really *make them study*, as they never before had studied when affiliated with the churches. Thus many Jehovah's Witnesses who once were ignorant Christians will say, "When I was a Christian I did not know the Bible as well as I do now." I come right back and say to them, "If you had studied as diligently in the Bible then as you study now in the *Watch Tower* books and the rigged New World translation of the Scriptures, you would have never fallen and have been over-reached by the devil." I know whereof I talk, for I am sad to report that I caused hundreds of Christians to stumble and fall. These had remained "babes in Christ" too long.

Let us face it, Christians: Most of our laymen are asleep, and are ignorant of the Bible. Because Christianity slacked in the proper use of Sunday, the Seventh Day Adventists' cult appeared with their Sabbath fetish and law and works righteousness; because Christianity ignored the healing aspect in the atonement, the Christian Science aberration appeared with its mental hocus pocus; because Christianity reneged on the tithing of time and money, the Mormons appeared with their gods and sex in heaven, stakes on earth, and controlled lives; because Christianity ceased in the persons of its so-called laymen to produce a witness for Christ, the Jehovah's Witnesses appeared with their misuse of witnessing in selling books. These cults are a WARNING. *They are the unpaid bills of Christianity.* They are here, because we failed. No hand-wringing and pious deprecation on their inroads will make them vanish. Unless our laymen become experts and Christian witnesses, we shall be "laughed out of the King's business." AWAKE, CHRISTIANS!

Remember, once before Christianity faced this problem. Paul describes it in Hebrews 5: 12-14, "For when for the time you ought to be teachers, ye have need that one teach you again which be the first principles of the oracles of God; and are become such as have need of milk, and not of strong meat. For everyone that useth milk is unskilful in the word of righteousness, for he is a babe. But strong meat belongeth to them that are of full age, even those who by reason of *use* have their senses exercised to discern both good and evil."

Scrutinize this charge carefully. First, all who are born-again Christians, Paul here implies, should reach the point of being able to teach Christianity to those who are lost, which is true *identity* in Christianity. Second, the initial period of instruction to a new believer in Christ is a limited one, and should culminate in growth in grace and truth in the knowledge of the Son of God (which is the universality or catholicity of the Church), where strong meat can be used. Third, each individual Christian must reach the point where by *use* his senses become exercised for good.

Examine Christian churches today. Behold how many "babes in Christ" we have. They cannot exercise their own senses in the *use* of Scripture; they have to be fed by others, with milk.

Note, this charge is not levelled against pastors, teachers and evangelists, who are set aside for the ministry of the Word. It is squarely levelled against what we today term "laymen". We have replaced the Scriptural name for all Christians who are not pastors, teachers and evangelists, which is *witness*, with "layman". What is the main charge levelled by Paul in Hebrews 5 against such so-called "laymen", or those who failed to witness for Christ? Such are "dull of hearing". That comes when, Sunday after Sunday, we sit in the house of God and have the Word of God expounded to us, and remain hearers only. We do not become *doers*, evangelizers and soul winners, or communicators or sharers of Christ with others. That is why we are like a man who looks in the mirror, sees his face, and then upon leaving the church quickly forget what we look like (James 1: 22–26). Lest we forget what we looked like we must, as Paul puts it in Hebrews 5, exercise our senses in *use*. Unless this practice of exercising our senses in *use of God's Word* for our growth in grace and truth of the knowledge of Jesus Christ is quickly restored, we shall fail.

How can we negate this fatal trend in our midst? Christians, awake! Christianity *lives* in witnessing, evangelizing and soul winning! Because this is so, learning becomes the first step in resolving the problem of our common salvation in others. Do we in Christianity regard it in this light? Are we, for that reason, hiding the Word of God in our hearts? Are we equipping ourselves by "studying to show ourselves approved"?

METHOD OF EVANGELIZING OR COMMUNICATING

(1 Cor. 11: 19; 2 Cor. 10: 3–5)

Coming from out of the background of the Jehovah's Witnesses, where God's Word already *in toto* is wrongly divided, and thus quite naturally becomes a "savour of death unto death" (2 Cor. 2: 16), it is most evident to me, that if we are to have the Word of God become a "savour of life unto life" (2 Cor. 2: 16) we must learn how "rightly to divide it" (2 Tim. 2: 15). In order to grow in grace toward manhood in Christ, we must have a steady supply of that "bread from heaven". Thus the work of evangelizing must start with us, in communicating Christ in us.

STEP ONE: *We must institute a systematic personal investigation of the Scriptures.*

Objections raised:
  (a) I have a bad memory.
  (b) The Bible is too large a book to read through.

Answering objections:
  (a) If you have a bad memory, then that is all the more reason to refresh it by reading the Bible all the way through

more often. Make it a life project. Memorize daily certain Scripture key-texts. One of the best ways to memorize such a key-text is to get a mental picture of the events, or truths, clearly in your mind, and then think of the key-verse you are memorizing as epitomizing this event or truth.

Confucius once said, "A picture is worth a thousand words." Once you have a mental picture to associate with the verse, you will never forget it. I remember in my early classes in German literature our teacher would always first paint a mental picture on the background association of the poem he was about to ask us to memorize. Once I got the picture, I remembered the poem. Memorize Scripture passages not like a parrot by repetition, but by picture thinking. Do this especially with salvation passages. It is fascinating. You become, in this manner, a "walking" Bible, or better still, since you are memorizing these passages because you want to use them for evangelizing, a "living" Bible. Peter, in 1 Peter 1: 23, suggested that we employ the Word of God that way. To make it live, or come to life *via* our lips.

(*b*) The Bible contains 1,189 chapters, and some of these consist of no more than two or three verses. If you read four chapters a day every weekday of the year, omitting Sundays, you will cover the entire Bible in one year with ease. Some people read three chapters in the morning and one chapter at night. Others prefer to read one chapter in the morning and three chapters at night. Whenever *you* retain more is the time to read it. If you do this faithfully every year, in ten, twenty, thirty, forty years your bad memory will have been entirely overcome, you will have grown. Often such a handicap is good, for someone once very aptly said, "A handicap can be a blessing when taken as a challenge." Your excuse of a bad memory, if you stop using it as an excuse and accept it as a challenge, can become *your* blessing.

Our memory is also a part of the marvellous adaptability we have in our bodies of flesh. I am reminded of the appearance of a young Greek at the Olympiads carrying a full-grown ox on his back the full length of the run. How could he do that? The explanation proved very simple. When the ox was but a little calf, the young Greek carried him every day the prescribed length. As the ox grew, so grew the Greek lad's strength of back and shoulders. Two years went by and the ox matured. But so had the strength of the Greek youth. Result: the feat described above.

The same, and much more, when we think of the way Peter puts it in 1 Peter 1: 22–24, can be done with the Word of God in faithful study of it every day. It will not only be something we carry adeptly on our shoulders, as did that Greek youth; it can become the LIVING WORD OF GOD, as it makes *you* a living witness and evangelizer.

STEP TWO: *We must institute personal studies in the Bible.*

Objections raised:

    (*a*) I lack the means to buy books.
    (*b*) I have no time.
    (*c*) I do not know how to organize a home Bible study.

Answering these objections:

(*a*) There isn't anybody in this twentieth century so poor that he cannot save a few pennies a day, by doing less munching of delicacies, or staying away from a few exhibitions, to raise the money. Parents, for instance, will do their children more good by building them a well-chosen library than by building for them a house.

Every Christian family should be furnished with at least one good exhaustive concordance, such as Cruden's, Young's or Strong's, a fine Bible Dictionary, such as Smith's or Unger's which are still fundamental *in toto*, and if possible a good commentary. For cult information, because in them is displayed two kinds of knowledge from experience, and because the cults today are our main challenge, you will find my two books very useful. Apart from being helpful soul winners, these books will do more: they will give you a wonderful insight into the excellency of what you have in Christianity, and what the cults have lost. This will help you in "speaking the truth in love" to these, and you will know exactly how to go about resolving their errors with truth spoken in love. What a blessing that will be.

A good Christian magazine should be subscribed for, and should be read. No Christian family should be without at least one such magazine. In these days of growing cults, the *Converted Jehovah's Witness Expositor* has become the hall mark of Christians who are setting out to win lost souls for Christ. Be sure to subscribe for it.

(b) You have no time? If you impose every evening but a two-hour TV black-out in your home, or just refrain once in a while from sitting in idle conversation about other people's things, you will have plenty of time. I travel constantly amidst Christian people, and know that everyone has time. Most of us work only an eight-hour day, five days a week. We never had so much leisure time. Our generation simply cannot use the excuse, "I have no time."

(c) The place to learn how to organize a home Bible study is in your church. However, I recommend the fine correspondence Bible courses put out by: (1) Lutheran Bible Institute, 13016 Greenwood ave. Seattle 33, Wash.; and (2) Moody's Bible Correspondence Courses, dept. 820 N La Salle St., Chicago 10, Ill. Both are very good systems: orthodox, well organized and effective. Write to either, or both, for a catalogue, and make your selection. These courses are practicable and orthodox, fundamental without modernist frills. Train yourself and your family in a family home Bible study.

You will be amazed how you will grow and advance in the "knowledge of our Lord Jesus Christ" in this manner. This Bible study period in your home with your family will become an enlivener of your personal Bible reading project, and a prompter *par excellence* for your memory and memorizing pictures.

STEP THREE: *We must have a complete practicable study system in our churches.*

Objections raised to this:

(a) It is hard to get a good attendance to a Bible study in a church during the week.

(b) Our Sunday-school classes cannot go into a systematic study of the Bible.

(c) With new ones coming in constantly, the study would never progress.

Answering these objections:

(a) If the Bible study organized in the church truly furnishes a platform of a social-type study discussion of the teachings of the select portions of the Word of God, it will be interesting. Such a study should review the Scriptural base for the doctrines we believe in. These studies should be slanted, to make necessary an actual going out into the neighbourhood to practise what has been learned. The teacher should thus not be a preacher, but rather a leader, and the chairman, doing as little talking as possible, merely sparking the discussions. Application and practicable inferences should be worked out, and these conclusions should then actually, under his guidance, be tested by putting them into communicating or evangelizing practices, thus making them suitable for the particular church's own views.

Also, remember the method you *use* here trains all participants in methods to *use* in their own home Bible studies; and, what is even more important, trains them how to handle home Bible studies in the homes of the people, with whom they have advanced from general witnessing to the personal contact in evangelizing and communicating Christ.

In harmony with this, then, as this study progresses, visiting parties should be organized; and one hour before the study commences these should actually go out and bring in new people.

The Bible study should end with a half-hour prayer meeting, which would become a well-rounded out mid-week meeting of the church. Here, intelligent, fervent prayer can be learned and practised, habitually enlisting the Lord's help for all pending evangelizing cases known to all in the study. Prayer should become the power house of this meeting, involving in scope: witnessing and studying. It will spark the habit of "praying without ceasing" (Phil. 4: 4–6; Eph. 6: 18–20; 5: 17); it will educate and promote method of prayer, and will culminate in an active participation as a labour of love in the kingdom of God (Rom. 15: 30). If taught and practised aright, and performed in this manner in prayer meetings, with each individual burdened because of their study and work, unity will ensue, effectiveness will appear, and prayers will be about proper things (Acts 1: 14; 4: 24; 12: 12). But more than that, this combination—witnessing, studying, prayer mid-week meeting of a church—will become a source of great power, or encouragement, and spiritual cleansing (Acts 4: 24–35), which will make the subsequent sermons on the Word of God by the pastor on the Sabbath more fruitful.

(*b*) Most churches today maintain departmental classes in Sunday-school. The fault in their *modus operandi*—and this is a cardinal one—is that the teachers talk too much. I have sat in innumerable classes, looking at well-prepared material, and have seen it completely ignored, while the teacher chewed, masticated and digested portions of it without giving the pupils a chance to do that.

Existing materials should be used inductively, and should be individualized; and if they are good materials, treating material universally, they should become identified with the individual in the process. Application should be made by reaching definite conclusions in the personal field, becoming established in identity. Lessons should actually be drawn. As conclusions are reached, incentives should be worked out, coupled with tasks assigned, to put all of this actually to work during the week, encouraging the individual to make his identity in the framework of the universality of the Church felt. Advanced groups should be formed from out of the above milieu, starting this process from age-brackets 12 and up, rewarding thus good marks denoting advance, in special Sunday-evening classes for advanced training. Proficiency, such as Philip, Stephen, and many others of the first Church attained, should here be emulated with constant zeal.

Objection (*c*) will be discussed graphically in chapter VI in the TRAINING, TEACHING AND TELLING plan.

Every church should have a well-stocked library containing good Christian books, and should subscribe to at least three Christian magazines. Just to bring out the value of a lending library, I want to say here that throughout the world former J.W.s now converted to Jesus Christ, and Christians, are using my two books as a means of contact with J.W.s. Some obtain the names and addresses of Jehovah's Witnesses and then go there and say, "I have a book here written by a former Jehovah's Witness which I would like you to read. If you promise to read it I would like to leave it here for ten days; then I shall return to pick it up. Should you like it, I will be glad to lend you then this man's second book." Hundreds of J.W.s have already been won this way to Christ. This same method, emanating from your church library, could be used in other fields, and with other books. Also from the church library a concerted effort should be made to furnish important books to your public libraries.

The church library should become the centre where reading, studying, witnessing, evangelizing and soul winning are automatically inculcated, taught and practised; where habits of this sort are formed, sustained and intelligently expanded in a loving way, to advance in grace and in the "knowledge of our Lord Jesus Christ."

Our Sunday-school among children, and courses for new-comers in our midst, are our hope for the future. We should train these to learn how to study, how to draw conclusions, how to *use* these conclusions.

These are cardinal steps in the direction of divine wisdom and advancement in "the knowledge of our Lord Jesus Christ." In practising them you will not only grow in grace yourself, but you will be trained to perform good work, the work of an evangelist (2 Tim. 4: 5) for Christ. Read your Bible, study the Word to make your approval manifest (1 Cor. 11: 19), by using every help you can lay your hands on. In this manner you will become prepared for the highest offices of usefulness of a Christian witness here, which are for the so-called layman: a proficient witness, evangeliser and soul winner; and when you reach the world to come you will be prepared to enter well equipped into a search for the unsearchable riches of the wisdom and knowledge of God.

PRACTICAL SUGGESTIONS

Witnessing for Christ, the "let your light shine" and the "Go ye therefore in all the world" type, is ADVERTISING CHRIST and the "new life in Christ". This is the broad approach of the means for salvation, as envisaged by the Lord in such terms as "broadcasting the seed, or Word of God", or "many are called, but few chosen." This would all be wasted unless we as Christians would advance from here, from the general approach to the specific, or to the personal contact. Evangelizing, as we discussed it in this chapter, because it is communicating, is that personal contact with such people whom we befriend for Christ. As is the case in our preparation consisting of reading, studying, praying, so now, as we make the personal contact with an interested party, we must follow through. Proverbs 27: 17, our Scripture for this discussion, shows the way: like this, "Iron sharpeneth iron: so a man sharpeneth the countenance of his friend." Here is the finest description of how you evangelize or communicate your personal contact: have a home Bible study with him.

There is only one exception to this rule: the Jehovah's Witness. He cannot be evangelized in a home Bible study, because he no longer has the true Word of God. With him, use *his* way of indoctrination: have a book study. Use my book *Into the Light of Christianity* for that study, because it is the only book written for that purpose and is compatible.

Harkening back to the years I worked with the NEW WORLD SOCIETY of Jehovah's Witnesses; Rutherford had just launched the WITNESSING FOR CHRIST advertising, with ADVERTISE, ADVERTISE, ADVERTISE THE KING AND THE KINGDOM, 1919–22, when the book method was introduced, and the witnessing or advertising began, and became centred in the offering for sale of books. Later this was augmented by other mass media: the convention, the radio and the gramophone. By 1935 we had put out hundreds of millions of books, advertised our brand of religion well; but we began to realize that we were not getting many converts. At that time I was in New York. I had been called there to enter Bethel. Also to become Company servant of Manhattan.

Remembering the effectiveness of this personal contact in Germany, where we had advanced much farther than had the Watchtower movement in America, I began to push for the evolvement of a method which would change the emphasis from mass witnessing with books, radio, etc., to the follow-up in a personal contact. At that time I met with similar views in the ranks of many advanced witnesses in the society. With the book *Riches*, we began use of the book study idea. Russell had already dabbled in that. But we gave it a totally different twist, and, advancing, we finally brought out the seven-step programme. This began to be used effectively from 1938, when in October of that year, the beginning of the THEOCRACY was hailed in Watchtower circles and a totalitarian top-down rule began to be enforced through and by means of the Zone-work. It is this personal contact which has made Jehovah's Witnesses formidable today.

In Christian circles we are still asleep here. Example: Billy Graham's mass meetings in Madison Square Garden. Large numbers of people appeared. It was good advertising. Many came forth to present themselves to the Lord. It was a good demonstration of "the new life in Christ", that is, as a beginning of it. Why didn't it at least turn out as successful as later did the huge convention of Jehovah's Witnesses held at the Yankee Stadium in 1958? The Watchtower reports that from August 1958 to January 1, 1960, or in one-and-a-half years, their units in the greater New York area had increased from 75 to 91 units. Just think of it, sixteen new congregations!

Some campaigns labour under the misunderstanding of what advertising Christ and what evangelising Christ denote. They are two different things. Peter and the early Church understood the difference between advertising Christ and evangelizing Christ. Just read Acts 2. First, note the pouring out of the Holy Spirit, the drawing of converts by the thousands, but then do not fail to see the follow-up especially described for us in Acts 2:46, "And they, continuing daily with one accord in the temple, and breaking bread from house to house, did eat their meat with gladness and singleness of heart." Their appreciation of the value of the personal contact was rewarded, because in the next verse we read, "Praising God, and having favour with the people. And the Lord added to the church daily such as should be saved."

The joining together in mass evangelism campaigns of many denominations with no common ground of policy or training of personnel leaves them open to confusion. Most Christian laymen and many churches ignore the witnessing work and the need for it by every believing Christian. It is a prerequisite in every campaign that the counsellors shall be trained witnesses for Christ who know how to evangelize, without this being so I conclude that they are ineffectual. Will this be seen and acted upon as quickly and effectively as the NEW WORLD SOCIETY reacted when they recognized the failure in 1935? Can it be true of our Christian brethren what the Lord said, "for the children of this world are wiser in their generation than the children of light" (Luke 16:8)? My next chapter "How to Win Souls for Christ". "Soul Winning is Sharing Our Surplus in Christ" will show that witnessing for Christ is only the beginning. May the Lord give us wisdom to see that.

LESSON SIX

The Story of the Personal Contact

Towards the end of the Lord's ministry on earth He entered and passed through Jericho. A huge crowd surrounded Him, as His fame had been noised about. A little fellow by the name of Zaccheus wanted very much to talk with Him. But there was no way he could reach the Lord.

However, he was a man of acumen and means, a tax collector, and thus a person who would not accept defeat. Up the sycamore tree he climbed (a rather unusual place for a man of means to be found) and the Lord saw him.

"Zaccheus, make haste, and come down; for today I must abide at thy house." In what a wonderful way the Holy Spirit worked in the heart of this man, on this remarkable day!

The Lord knew instantly: this *is* the time for a personal contact. The work of the Holy Spirit had begun on the spirit of this son of Abraham. A sinner he was, despised by the Jews, rich; but the immediate result, i.e. the outward result, of the Lord's contact with Zaccheus was this statement: "Behold, Lord, the half of my goods I give to the poor; and if I have taken anything from any man by false accusation, I restore him fourfold."

Zaccheus had become spiritual-minded, the Lord had lit his spirit, which is the candle of the Lord, and graciously the Lord says: "This day is salvation come to this house, for as much as he also is a son of Abraham."

Remarkable things can happen to you, Christian, if, as a witness for Christ, you noise the Gospel of Jesus Christ about. Sooner or later the Holy Spirit will guide you into places *you* could never have discerned by just cursorily as a deacon, or an elder, or a team of church workers, making what today is called "visitations" designed to keep in touch with your members.

AN OLD STORY

You may say, Jesus was an exception in practising personal contacts. Open up your Bible at Genesis 13:18 and let us read, "So Abram moved his tent, and came and dwelt by the oaks of Mamre, which are at Hebron; and there he built an altar to the Lord."

Mamre is the proper name of a man, just as Zaccheus was. Notice, this scripture therefore speaks of, and delineates for us, a personal contact made by Abraham with a man called Mamre.

In Genesis 14: 13 we are told he was an Amorite, of a breed who later became despised, as despised as were the tax-collectors in Jesus' day.

Mamre, like the rich among us, lived in the country near the famous city of Hebron, which had in its neigh-bourhood a wood or an oak grove. At Mamre's place Abraham, the witness who perambulated up and down the country of Canaan, was hospitably received with his entire house.

Here was evidence of need for Abraham's ministry, and a personal contact was in order. Observe how Abraham goes about it. Moses takes special care to mention here that at Mamre's Abraham built an altar to the Lord, i.e. preached and gave instructions about the true worship of God.

WE CARRY THE BLESSEDNESS OF CHRIST WITH US

To us, who live in a world filled with dead orthodoxy, modernism, atheism, this is no small comfort, that God gathers remnants from the heathen and lets them partake of the blessing of Abraham.

How wonderful for us Witnesses for Christ, who have found grace and peace and every blessing in Christ, to realize that even at that time, so far back, God had His worshippers among the heathen. These were worshippers whom God called in a marvellous manner through Abraham, in accord-ance with the promise given him in Genesis 12: 3, "You shall be a blessing", that is, the blessing inherent in you that, wherever you may come, others will also receive a blessing through your ministry.

Because, Christian, you have the grace and truth of the knowledge of Jesus Christ, you are the logical one not only to be a Witness for Christ, but if you are faithful in this phase, as Abraham was in walking up and down Canaan, and Jesus was up and down Galilee and Judea, then the Lord will use you, by giving you personal contacts, where the real work of grace is done.

That is why Jesus, who knew how much blessedness you would carry in you, said long ago to His disciples, "If the house is worthy, let your peace come upon it" (Matt. 10: 13).

PERSONAL CONTACT BRINGS PEACE

The human race, living on a rapidly ageing earth which is headed for destruction, are in a peculiarly verdant condition of common grace, with special grace in Jesus Christ beckoning, as we read in Acts 17: 27, 28.

At any moment a human may, as Zaccheus did, reach the point, where the grace of God reaches him, where He suddenly recognizes the need of a Saviour. If you are about your "Father's business" of being "a Witness for Christ" (Acts 1: 8), the Lord will show you where to make the personal contact, so that your blessedness in Christ can be shared.

Whenever the Holy Spirit turns a man from his flesh, and makes him look inward on his spirit, the moment has arrived for the Lord to light that man's candle.

We read in Proverbs 20: 27, "The spirit of man IS THE CANDLE of the Lord, searching all the inward parts of the belly."

Attracted by the spiritual GOSPEL of Jesus Christ, or your testimony, which sometimes may take many years, at some stage, YOU, who bear the gospel, will shine out to a lost one, and He will invite you in. Immediately you will sense his spiritual need, as did Abraham with Mamre, and Jesus with Zaccheus. You will let your peace come upon that house (Matt. 10: 13).

SHARPENING THE COUNTENANCE

With such an opening, what sort of a personal contact is this to become? A social one? Where you cultivate a fleshly relationship? NO.

In order to avoid falling into the pitfalls of the flesh, be wise, think of this contact in the following terms: "Iron sharpeneth

iron; so a man sharpeneth the countenance of his friend"
(Prov. 27: 17).

Glancing around, in order to find a proper programme for
such a contingency, we wonder what is the proper *modus
operandi* for a personal contact. Just visiting? Just making
social calls in order to show by such a contact that, as represent-
atives of our church, we display what a wonderful association
we have? Obviously, such procedure does not fill the purpose
of the personal contact, which, as we recall, is, "to light the
candle of man's spirit". There is only one way to light a man's
spirit, and that is the way Abraham did it, and the Lord did
it. With the Word of God.

A BIBLE STUDY IS THE IDEAL M.O. FOR A PERSONAL CONTACT

Without God's written Word there would be no God
in our hearts. For God is only there, where there is a
knowledge of His word. To the Word of God, then, and its
study!

But you may reply, I do not know how to lead a study in
the Bible. True, most organization Christians today do not
know. That is why Jehovah's Witnesses, Seventh Day Adventists, and others can come in the name of the Lord, i.e.
with the Word of God watered down in their books, and start
Book studies in the homes of the people.

Let us begin to train ourselves, right now. As you read in
this entire chapter, there is only one way. Have someone in
your church start a congregational Bible study, to be held
once a week. Select a good correspondence Bible study on
either of the four gospels. Each night go through one
lesson. Train yourself to handle this lesson expertly. As
you progress, *you* will be able to take that correspondence
course to your personal contact, and have an exact study
with them. The oftener you do that, the more expert you
will become.

But all the time you are *using* the Word of God, and your
testimony of the saving grace in Jesus Christ. The two
will not only light the candle of your contact, but they will
receive fuel and will grow, and soon the Lord, in and through
the Holy Spirit, will convert such a soul right before your
eyes.

When that happens, salvation has come to that house (Luke 19: 1–9; Gen. 13: 18) to save (in personal contacts) "that which is lost" (Luke 19: 10). This blessedness inherent in the Lord's work and gospel is also in you, and He says to you, "If the house is worthy, let your peace come upon it" (Matt. 10: 13).

CHAPTER V

HOW TO WIN SOULS FOR CHRIST

SOUL-WINNING: A SHARING OF OUR SURPLUS IN CHRIST

"THE fruit of the righteous is a tree of life; and he that winneth souls is wise," is echoed by our Lord Jesus Christ in Luke 13: 6–9 in the parable about a whole nation planted to bear fruit: "He spake also this parable; a certain man had a fig tree planted in a vineyard; and he came and sought fruit thereon, and found none. Then said he unto the dresser of his vineyard; Behold, these three years I come seeking fruit on this fig tree, And find none; cut it down: why cumbereth it the ground? and he answering said unto him, Lord, let it alone this year also, till I shall dig about it, and dung it: and if it bear fruit, well: and if not, then after that thou shalt cut it down." When, finally, it appeared so evident that fruit was not forthcoming, we hear the Lord's word in Matthew 21: 43, "Therefore say I unto you, the kingdom of God shall be taken from you, and given to a nation bringing forth the fruits thereof."

Thus we of Christianity have fallen heir to the kingdom of God by grace. What are we bringing forth: fruits or works? The Jewish nation concentrated on works righteousness, and therefore failed to produce fruits. It was rejected. Great was their surplus in God, heaped generously upon them in the past. Still greater is our surplus heaped upon us in Christ. What are we doing about it?

FAITH OR WORKS: WHICH?

Faith in the righteousness of God cannot exist in connection with works. Justification by works, of whatever character they may be, are therefore incompatible as a source for the righteousness of God. To claim both, faith and works, as the source of it, would be the same as "limping with two different opinions" (1 Kings 18:21). It is like worshipping Baal, and kissing one's own hand (Job 31:27, 28).

Going back to my last years as a Jehovah's Witness and being a full-time servant of the Watch Tower Society, and my first years of being a Christian, I remember this: from the moment I began to have faith, I learned in my soul that all things in me were altogether blameworthy, sinful and damnable. I began to understand Romans 3:23, since "all have sinned and fallen short of the glory of God"; and Romans 3:10-12 came clear to me as it chimed into my consciousness these words: "None is righteous, no, not one . . . all have turned aside, together they have gone wrong."

It took me a whole thirty years to learn that. Year after year, from my sixteenth year to my forty-seventh year, I had piled up a record of works: at seventeen I converted a score to the movement in Berlin; at nineteen I began training for the ministry; at twenty-one I was giving public lectures before thousands, and had already achieved proud martyrdom in being beaten and jailed, in deflecting mobs in the town of Rathenau in Germany. From 1932 on, in the U.S.A. I worked in over thirty states of the Union as a pioneer, building up the NEW WORLD SOCIETY. Then in 1935 I was called to New York, became Company servant there, was placed in charge of the pioneer desk at headquarters, which was the key position for the missionary work in the U.S.A. I helped develop the seven steps, led in legal fights, became Zone servant, and acted as personal representative of Judge Rutherford in the Midwest. In this work I was stoned and mobbed. When in the night of my awakening, April 18th, 1952, the Lord broke this record by being ready to chop it and myself down, my soul learned early that morning this, *I knew that I needed Christ*, who had suffered, died and risen for me so that, believing on Him, I might become a new man—a man who bears fruits, instead of performing works. To what extent? In so far as my sins were forgiven, and I became justified by the merit of another, namely, my Lord Jesus Christ.

What a turning point that became to me! For thirty years as a Jehovah's Witness, taking the lead effectively in that association, I had piled up the above-mentioned record, which had been kept at headquarters in Magdeburg, Germany, and Brooklyn, N.Y. But now this wonderful experience with my Lord Jesus Christ taught me that my soul, or inner man, could only be ruled by faith (Rom. 10: 10). I understood then that the inner man, or soul, could only be justified, freed and saved by faith; and that no kind of works had anything at all to do with my soul.

How could this be? came the query from my J.W. background. This puzzled me. I knew that ungodliness, selfishness and unbelief of heart, without outer good works in evidence, were still condemned in the body of flesh, and that their lack would brand me as a servant of sin.

My first concern now, however, as a soul, became to lay aside all the confidence I had had in my thirty years of works in the Jehovah's Witness system of things. Pressing on, I had increasingly to strengthen my faith so that I could *grow through such faith* in grace, in the knowledge of Jesus Christ, who suffered, died and rose for me (1 Pet. 5: 10).

Here we come face to face with soul-winning. It works first in us, then Christ in and through us in others. How? As we comply in obedience to the commands and promises in Christ, who works in and through us by the Holy Spirit.

No other work makes a Christian, or wins a soul. How emphatically the Lord Jesus Christ brushed aside the Jewish, flesh-conditioned question "What must we do to be doing the work of God," by saying, "This is the work of God, that you believe in him whom he has sent" (John 6: 28, 29).

Soul-winning is the result of faith and obedience, then. It finds by these fruits its first success in our own souls, as the work of God. Thus you see, a fruit after the Spirit is not a work done by us, but becomes the *work of God* through us. We are thus made a spectacle for men and angels, of God at work in and through us (1 Cor. 4: 9).

A TREASURE BEYOND COMPARE

True faith in Christ, setting us onto our course of action which displays us as a tree bearing such fruit, is thus a treasure beyond comparison. It saves a man from every evil. It brings in a salvation great and free (Mark 16: 16).

Isaiah thought about this treasure. Let us read what his thoughts were in Isaiah 10, "The Lord will make a small and consuming work upon the land, and it will overflow with righteousness." Faith is at first small but perfect fulfilment of the law. But, as Isaiah depicts, it ushers in "the whole work of God" (v. 10). In reading the whole context of Isaiah 10, note that, small though the beginning is, it will fill the believer with so great a righteousness that nothing henceforth will ever be needed by him to become righteous. That is why Paul says, "For man believes with his heart, and so is justified" (Rom. 10: 10).

The power unto salvation in the gospel of Jesus Christ, therefore, is faith. How different this is to coming from the so-called "gospel of the kingdom" preached by the Jehovah's Witnesses, or by the social gospels of foolish ones I hear so much about in the halls of liberalism.

From the viewpoint of reason, my mind once trained in work righteousness, asks: Is this not a paradox? How can faith alone justify; and by it, how can we be offered such great treasure without works? Are not so many works, ceremonies and laws prescribed in the Scriptures?

The entire Scripture of God, I learn upon reflection and study, really has two parts (Gal. 4: 22–28): commandments and promises. Commandments teach me what is good and what I ought to do. They do not give me the power to do it.

COMMANDMENTS REVEAL OUR HELPLESSNESS

Man has gone astray, and in his soul he no longer knows himself. Some have gone so far, and I had been one of them as a Jehovah's Witness, as to deny they have a soul. Commandments in this situation have a very valid purpose: they are given to men to help us know ourselves. It is through the commandments that we recognize our inability to do good. That is why commandments are called the Old Testament or Covenant.

Let me depict just one example as to how a commandment works. Example: "Thou shalt not covet" (Exod. 20: 17). This commandment, in the final analysis, proves every one of us a sinner. Who of us can avoid coveting, no matter how much we struggle against it? In desperation we finally seek elsewhere. "Destruction is your own, O Israel: your help is in me" (Hos. 13: 9) already cries out. This goes for all commandments.

But inability to perform and keep the law notwithstanding, the commandments *must* be fulfilled. When man recognizes his helplessness, and begins to wonder anxiously how he can fulfil the law, he becomes humbled. He is thus reduced in his own eyes. In himself he can find nothing reassuring whereby he may be saved. I learned that in a whole night of prayer, on April 18th, 1952, beginning in the evening backed with what I considered a fine record of works; but as the night wore on into morning, I had become totally reduced in my own eyes. I became humbled, so humbled that I threw myself upon the Lord and cried out, "Lord have mercy, I am a sinner, forgive me." I was saved immediately thereafter.

PROMISES TAKE OVER

Thus utter disability which results in condemnation, as the law must be fulfilled in full, every jot and tittle thereof, brings the second part of the Scriptures into brilliant contrastive view. This is not a theological description, but actually happened to myself—and since, I have learned, has happened to many, many others who were born again.

It is the promises of God against the backdrop of his commandments, which declares the glory of God. All of this is economically incorporated in the gospel of Jesus Christ. Its power unto salvation, therefore, is not by works. It is by faith.

If you are one of those who already know you fail to fulfil the law, and are not kidding yourself by claiming that you are keeping the law, and know it, but wish to do it very much, the promises of God ask you to believe in Jesus Christ who is our righteousness, peace, liberty, and who became all promised goodness to us. The offer is, "If you believe, you shall have all things; if you do not believe, you shall lack them." That is the gist of Isaiah 10, alluded to above.

All that through many works you tried to accomplish but failed miserably to do you will accomplish at once through faith. This actually *is* God's will, who makes all things in the flesh depend on faith. This is not a dream. It is not a fairy-tale I am relating to you to entertain you. Read of it in God's Word, in Romans 11:32, "For God has consigned all men to disobedience, that He may have mercy upon all."

You see, then, how the promises of God give what the commandments of God demand? Therefore, and teaching this to lost ones is *the art of soul-winning*; both the commandments and the fulfilment of the commandments, are God's alone.

THAT IS THE NEW TESTAMENT—it is this wonderful array of truths, which must be preached or witnessed to, sounded down or communicated into their ears, and demonstrated in soul-winning, by everyone who is saved, to those who are still lost. It is imperative we do this, and that we quickly forget about being laymen becoming Christian witnesses. Christians, awake! It means so much.

NEW TESTAMENT WAY OF PREACHING

The New Testament way brings to view the "new life in Christ" being impressed upon the inner man (Eph. 2: 8–10), according to the promises of God, and is therefore a positive, soul-winning ministry *usward*, and expands outwardly towards other souls. We become, as Paul says in Ephesians 2, in salvation, examples to others, as Christ becomes in salvation our example.

God's purposes are holy, true, righteous, free, peaceful words, goodness. The soul which firmly clings to these promises in faith magically will be totally absorbed by them. Not only will it share these promises, but in sharing them it itself will become saturated and even intoxicated with them. Instead of the brain, the heart will begin to speak of Jesus and His love.

Faith is the power. If a touch of the Lord Jesus healed, how much more will His tender spiritual touch, this absorbing in faith of the Word, communicate to the soul all things that belong to the Word. How wonderfully Peter puts this in 1 Peter 1: 18–25.

Soul-winning, then, in essence, is a display of our new relationship by use of the language of our heart and use of our bodies, to touch in goodness lost ones. But all who believed in His name, "He gave power to become the sons of God" (John 1: 12). It is thus *faith* alone, and without any works whatever, which justifies the soul, sanctifies it, and makes it true, peaceful, free and filled with every blessing in Jesus Christ through the Word of God.

Can you see from what source faith derives so great a power, which the greatest works cannot top? It is quite evident that God has decreed that faith and the Word of God alone shall rule the soul. In this way God implants His "image and likeness" into the soul. Thus, you see, no good work can even claim the Word of God for sanction. Much less can a good work *live* in a soul. The body of man was formed out of existing things. The soul of man, however, was created by God with "the breath of lives" (Gen. 2: 7). The qualities of the Word of God alone bring life to the soul, for both the soul and the Word of God are spiritual.

HONOURING GOD IN CHRIST BRINGS LIBERTY

It is true, then, that the "law is not laid down for the just" (1 Tim. 1: 9). A Christian has all he needs in faith. But this Christian liberty, which is really the depth of our faith, does not induce us to live in idleness and wickedness, but simply makes the law and works unnecessary for man's righteousness and salvation.

We have everything for salvation in faith. It is the first and overriding aspect. But faith without honouring God would be dead.

The second aspect of faith honours Him whom it trusts. That is evident because it considers Him truthful and trust-worthy. As our soul firmly trusts in God's promises, never doubting them, it regards Him as truthful and righteous. You cannot ascribe anything more excellent to God. This is the very highest worship of God if we ascribe truthfulness and righteousness to Him by carrying our faith to the obedience of confessing it to others as an act of worship.

Once the soul reaches this transcendent stage of faith, which is an outreach to others, it unlocks the door to the imprinting of the "image of God" in its soul: for in doing this, the soul in a most positive manner to witness, by the praises of its lips, speaking the language of its new heart, consents to do His will. *From that moment on it is won by God:* for it hallows His name then instinctively, and allows itself willingly to be treated according to God's will and pleasure.

Clinging thus to God's promises, you see, it does not doubt that He who is true, just, wise, will do and provide all things well. This is the transcendent freedom in Christ. Why?

The obedience of the soul is by faith. Such obedience therefore has truly fulfilled every commandment. There is no greater fulfilment than by the obedience of faith. Not works of faith: yes, obedience of faith.

DISHONOURING GOD BY LIVING A SILENT, DORMANT LIFE

You say that you have faith? You say that you are saved? I ask, do you trust God? Trust Him enough to go out of your camp or church circle, and tell others about your God? Or have you just "grasped" at salvation for your *self*, and are now chanting religiously, "I am saved", going off by yourself in some corner of your home, or into a conspicuous place in the circle of your church, singing songs to yourself; humming, humming holy tunes, *keeping so great a salvation all to yourself*? Are you afraid, perhaps, although you would not come out and admit it, that it is perhaps too good to be true? Or, worse still, secretly do you perhaps not trust God to be truthful, at least not enough to go out and admit it and go out and shout "from the housetops, what you hear in the secret place" (Matt. 10: 27), or to "confess with your mouths" what in your hearts you already "believe unto salvation"? (Rom. 10: 10).

If you are not actually practising this second stage of faith, look out! For this could be tantamount to contempt of God —this not fully trusting Him. Such inactivity, in any case, spells out distrust of God. Face it, Christian: Awake! You cannot just be a layman and be "alive in Christ"; you are either a layman or an expert: which?

Remember Abraham? Only after he left Haran, the in-between place, and actually came forth to live in the strange land of promise, did he truly show his trust in God. In that way he worshipped God by greatly honouring Him as a trustworthy God.

If you curtail the outreach of God through you, who already were reached by His love, your worship will stagnate, eddy inside of you, and you will begin to set up an idol in your heart. Forever after, once you have stagnated thus into inactivity, will you chant, "I am saved, I am saved," giving eloquent testimony that you are selfishly concerned with yourself. When you thus chant, are you not chanting worship of yourself as *that* important "I AM SAVED, I, I"? Never forget, Christian, that your salvation comes from God, and fills your heart with such a righteousness that you cannot help thereafter, once the Lord has come into your heart and filled it to confess it with your lips. In that way you reach out to help others, showing your trust in your God and in His promises. Only with your lips do you worship God. Otherwise, if you are silent about the matter, or, worse still, are a chanter of "I am saved, I am saved", denoting you are worshipping the idol *self* in your heart. Instead of perambulating with joyful feet bringing tidings of good, you are carrying around a dead worship without results in winning others, always only remaining "a layman".

But more than that. To remain silent, not to witness, not to communicate or evangelize this faith to others, not to enter upon a career of soul-winning, *is* disobedience, and displays a definite lack of trust in God. Such failures are Laodicean in character, and are far worse than anger and lust of the flesh. That is why they are not included under lust and anger, for such were cleansed of these. Such have had the offer to be cleansed, and shrink back from coming all the way and paying their vows—they are like Lot's wife, they freeze into a salt-stick-like unproductivity. All such are categorically included under the sin of unbelief.

Do you believe in Christ? Is His righteousness yours? Did you come by it through faith? Fine. Come now, if you are only a layman, you have only come halfway. Come out of Haran. Come into the open. Come into the strange land of promise, and worship God in "spirit and in truth". Become an expert, be a WITNESS FOR CHRIST! Evangelize, by doing it yourself in communicating your salvation in this manner. Do not rely on others, other Christians to do it for you. They have their own witnessing to do. YOU be a soul-winner. Pay God this great honour in being a witness, an evangelizer, a soul-winner. Give Him in this way YOUR faith and trust, and YOU will be greatly honouring Him. Observe, if you honour God in His glory of being a truthful and trustworthy God, God will glorify your righteousness by giving you much increase in your witnessing, evangelizing and soul-winning work. God is truthful. God is just.

Consider Him, and confess Him in this way to be, and YOU will be truthful and just. Accordingly we read, "Those who honour me I will honour, and those who despise me shall be lightly esteemed" (1 Sam. 2: 30). Abraham's faith was reckoned to him as righteousness (Rom. 4). Why? Because in going into the land of Canaan, the land of promise, by faith, he gave God glory most perfect. How? By adding obedience to his faith. Obedience to God because he trusted Him, his God. For this very same reason shall our faith be reckoned to us as righteousness, if *we believe and obey.*

COMPLETE UNITY OF FAITH

Obedience added to faith leads to the incomparable benefit of unity of faith. It is in this manner that the soul is united with the Lord Jesus Christ as a bride is united with her bridegroom. By this secret (we read of it in Eph. 5: 31, 32), Christ and our soul become one flesh.

Here now we have the perfect truth. By the nature of things, the soul and our Lord Jesus Christ now have everything in common. This embraces both the good and the evil. The soul thus can boast and glory in whatever Christ Jesus has, as though it were its own. On the other side, whatever the soul has, our Lord Jesus Christ claims as His own.

Stop with me here for just a moment. Let us think this out. Let us compare this connubial bliss which a unity of faith projects:

(1) Christ is full of grace, life and salvation.
(2) The soul is full of sin, death and condemnation.

Can *you* measure the blessings of unity of faith in Christ Jesus in this third phase of faith accruing to the soul? Can I excite you, if you are not doing this yet, to go forth from faith to faith by obedience, coming thus intimately in faith with Christ? Can't you see, "the measure you have received from Christ" (Eph. 4: 7) is to be a witness for Christ, as the measure for a pastor is to be a shepherd in Christ? You cannot be a layman in this relationship and live up to your "measure in Christ". Here is how you do it practically, to wit:

(1) Witnessing to your faith in Christ Jesus to others (that is your measure).

(2) Evangelizing or communicating with others, adding the obedience of a messenger (that is your growth in grace and truth).

(3) Soul winning by drawing, by your example, into a unity of faith in Christ, which leads invariably to fruitfulness in bringing increase, as a wife brings to a husband. (This is your reaching the maturity of the stature of a man in Christ.)

Christ is God and man in one person. As God He cannot

sin, or be condemned, for His righteousness, life and salvation are eternal and omnipotent. As a man He died, and by faith He shares in the sins, death and pains of hell, which are ours, His bride's. In doing this, death and the grave couldn't swallow Him up. On the contrary. He swallowed up death and the grave. Why? His righteousness is greater than all the sins of all men. He has the kind of life which is stronger than death. Yes, His salvation is more transcendent than hell!

What does unity in faith in Christ bring?

(1) The troth of the believing soul brings freedom in Christ.
(2) Brings freedom from sin in it.
(3) Brings security against death and the grave.
(4) Endows it with everlasting life, the eternal righteousness of Christ its bridegroom (Eph. 5: 26, 27; Hos. 2: 19, 20).

Who now of us, so wedded with Christ Jesus in faith, can fully appreciate the riches of the glory of His grace? Read this by-play of Scripture on this epochal unity of faith: Song of Solomon 2: 16; 1 Corinthians 15: 57 and then, verse 56.

After all is said and done, this one great fact leaps forth to view: *Faith in its most advanced stage can fulfil the first commandment:* THOU SHALT WORSHIP ONE GOD. God can only be worshipped in ascribing to Him the glory of truthfulness and all goodness (Exod. 34: 6; Ps. 27: 13; 31: 19; 52: 1; Zech. 9: 17; Rom. 11: 22). *Such worship is not performed by works.* It is rendered by faith in the heart, and translated by obedience through the lips. By believing do we glorify God, and by adding obedience to that faith do we acknowledge that He is truthful and good, worshipping Him. Thus, you see, this first commandment must be fulfilled before any works whatever can be done. Any works whatever, proceed through obedience from the fulfilment of this commandment.

GRACE TO THE INNER MAN IN CHRIST

The position of the first-born was highly prized in Old Testament times. At best, however, it was only typical. This position, in all of its rich meaning, became a reality to us who are "in Christ". In the family of Israel the first-born held by birthright the implicatory duties of king and priest. Implied though they were, they became later centred in the tribe of Levi, as far as the priesthood became concerned. But lo, in

Christ, the two prerogatives of king and priest are His by birth-right once again. Because of the souls' marriage with our Lord Jesus Christ, He imparts and shares these prerogatives with all who believe (1 Pet. 2: 7).

Note, the inversion—or, better, expansion? The highly-prized position of the first-born contracts in Israel, to be sure, to one tribe, that of Levi. In Christ, since these prerogatives of being the first-born of God are His by birthright, this soon expands to all who have no right to it whatever, and this comes about by faith.

"Kingly" indeed is the subjection by faith in Christ, which by the way is our salvation (Rom. 8: 28; 1 Cor. 3: 21–23). But "priestly" also it becomes, with suffering, evils to endure, which become ours in Christ too (2 Cor. 12: 9; Rom. 8: 28). To endure both is the inestimable power and liberty of Christians, *who are awake as witnesses for Christ, and not asleep as laymen.* For in it both, the subjection of Christ and in the enduring of evil, and in it all, we come ACTIVELY with boldness into the presence of God (Heb. 10: 19–22) and pray ABBA, FATHER! If we are asleep as laymen, chirping half-wittedly, "I am saved, I am saved", our prayer would be a mockery and a "strange fire" and, as this wrong worship once brought death to Aaron's sons who practised it, it would burn us out, leaving only the outer garments of a profession of being members of some church. But because of our subjection and our endurance becoming *real* as witness for Christ, we pray not only for ourselves, we also pray for one another, and do all things which we saw done and foreshadowed in the visible work of priests; and we become in fact, when we reach the stature of manhood in Christ (Eph. 4: 14), a whole "chosen generation, a royal priesthood" (1 Pet. 2: 9). To such glory man can certainly not come by his works, but by his faith alone (Phil. 4: 13).

To illustrate how the power of faith in Christianity works in this manner, let me quote an experience I had when but a lad of seventeen. Although I was already partially a Russellite at that time, still I was a witnessing Christian *per se.* I was able to feel for the woman in question, and, feeling, was able to generate in my heart ALL the fear she had. But, unlike her, I was able to fall onto my knees and pray for her, believing the Father would help. The occasion, the sympathy, the ministry, the prayer, were all present, and the DEMONS LEFT THE WOMAN.

Read of this experience and its context in my book *Thirty Years a Watch Tower Slave*, page 17, paragraph 2.

Is it any wonder, then, as we grow in grace that we ought to preach Christ crucified, and arisen: the cross; to the end that faith in Him may be established? If in the above way of retardation the Lord blessed the woman, what could happen to sick, maimed, worried persons, if some Christian could feel for them so genuinely Samaritan-like, that suddenly the unselfishness of it all, the power of faith in the Christian heart, the Holy Spirit beginning to fructify it, could bring about a work of God in the conversion, a new birth, and in a healing; soul winning *is* that way! The weakness of man *is* God's Opportunity and strength, if we Christians but *use* it that way. What a blessing we can be in this twentieth century!

This spells out, unlike that somnambulent layman's refrain, "I am saved, I am saved", which echoes so loudly and confusingly throughout Christendom today, to her shame and drowsiness, not only, "Christ in me." No, much more, if we Christians but awake: Christ in you and me. That will do it. Such a boon can only be conferred upon others by witnessing why our Lord Jesus came, what He brought and what He bestows. Make clear what the benefits will be if we accept Him as our personal saviour: it will bring us into the universality of the Church with a new-creation personal identity for all eternity. From out of your believing heart, Christian, become an expert in this milieu: refuse to be considered a layman. From this wide-awake position tell the magic, moving story of Jesus Christ becoming our righteousness. *Make it simple, and tell it often.* Tell of how faith fulfils all impossible obstacles. Tell exactly how things were with you. Tell how your Saviour changed your hopeless condition. Confess Jesus Christ as your Saviour. Give Him full credit, but never fail to tell of the magic of faith, which is the power unto salvation in the gospel of Jesus Christ.

This approach is very good if you, as a good listener, fully synchronized your feelings and sympathies with the ailments, troubles, sins, shortcomings, of your contact. When he knows that you feel for him after you have done good to him, spent time with him, practicably helped him with food, goods, advice, doing things for him he could not do for himself, you must then *translate* your sympathy as already displayed in what you did for him so far in the body into the spiritual realm.

By following through here with your testimony, backing it up with your prayer, focus his attention upon his sins. Lead him to repentance, and, when it comes, quickly step in with the promises of Christ.

To illustrate. Recently, at the end of one of my meetings in a church, a J.W. came to me, fully set upon arguing with me. I patiently answered her questions. She thanked me as she raised others, and decided to shake my hand which she had refused at the outset. I held on to her hand, my heart in my eyes, and said, "Sister, I haven't helped your soul, have I?" She replied, "What do you mean?" I said, "You know, all of this, arguments, Scriptural understanding, is really putting the cart before the horse. If you come repentantly to the Lord, and let Him come into your heart, then the heavens will be opened to you, and you will have no trouble understanding the Bible." By this time there was that stricken look in her eyes which told me quite clearly that she was concerned. I moved in fast now, and with confidence, saying, "Do you know how Christ can come into your heart?" She said, "No. Can you show me?" I replied, "Let us read Revelation 3: 20, and, looking it up, began to read the verse.

Puzzlement on her face for a minute. Quickly I moved in to dispel that by saying, "Come, kneel with me," and began to pray as a "king" and a "priest", a fellow-heir with Christ, with complete confidence and authority and faith. "Lord, hear us; show this woman how that if she hears your knock at the door of her heart at this moment, that she finds grace to open her heart; Lord, do more: give her the ability to believe that you will enter at once into her heart, if she voices this invitation with her own lips, in full faith." Stopping, I said, "Sister, the Lord is waiting for your invitation."

A few minutes went by—I wondered. Then, beautifully sincere, came a childlike prayer from her lips, "Lord, forgive my sins, cleanse my heart, let your righteousness be mine, and come now into my heart. Amen." She arose with a radiant smile on her face, fully assured that the Lord was in her heart. She was saved. Here, note the lecture, her objections to some remarks thereof, sympathy on my part shown her in patiently answering her many questions, and then quick action in soul-winning brought salvation. *That is how soul-winning works.* You have to prepare for it, trusting in the Lord to step in at the right moment, as the Holy Spirit gives the nudge.

There are other approaches which will have to be used if obvious sins, or heresies, sicknesses, worries and troubles do not appear. If over a period of time you have been evangelizing a person in a personal contact by use of a Bible study, you will have to begin translating slowly your approach from the mind to the heart, from different angles lucidly bringing your testimony to this person's attention. Be sympathetic. Come to him in a very pleasing way, pleasing him. Paul once said, ". . . I am all things to all men, if perchance I might win them for Christ". Accommodate yourself to a person's needs, or to his outlook. Notice how the good Samaritan worked? It is said by some that the good Samaritan did not follow through. But this is a parable, and the Lord wanted to show a specific point. But in other cases the Lord watched sympathetically for the evidence of interest, and then moved in fast as a personal contact. Remember Zacchaeus, sitting atop of a sycamore tree? Seeing him, the Lord moved most directly by saying he would see him later at his home. . . . This kind of quick discernment, follow-up and personal contact, must follow, once you have entered into personal contact. Overwhelm him with your goodwill and intentions, and he will not long resist your efforts enriched with your recital of the good that will come to him. He will begin seriously to consider such possible boons. After all, he has the same type of body in common with you. Receiving much tender comfort from you, he will also grow tender, and will slowly begin to love *your* Lord Jesus Christ. He will begin to discern that you who were so much like him in the flesh became this way, this pleasing way, because you are "in Christ". Never could you have brought him to love your Lord Jesus Christ by any kind of works you might have taught and trained him to perform. How well I know this. How many thousands of Jehovah's Witnesses did I once train in the works of becoming Kingdom Publishers to become efficient witnesses, and who never came to love our Lord Jesus Christ and to find salvation, and are now "twice condemned". O Lord, have mercy on me, and upon those whom I misled.

Even in the half-sphere of works-faith as a missionary for Jehovah's Witnesses, I had become expert in making myself all things to all men in order to sell them Watch Tower books, and saw it work. Once, assigned in a count in the eastern U.S.A., I came upon a large area occupied by a group known as Amish. Driving my model A Ford, I vainly tried for three days to contact these people in order to sell them Watch Tower books. Everywhere I was turned down, and that curtly. I had had opposition before, many doors being shut, often yards closed to me; but in *every place*, that had never happened. I was puzzled. That evening I engaged an old-timer in conversation and asked, "Why do Amish people refuse me to drive onto their yards and offer them Bibles and books?" He told me that they had an aversion to cars, and most likely because I said I preached they were especially down on me.

I saw he had one of those Amish buggies, and asked him, "Could you rent me that buggy and a horse?" He looked at me queerly and said, "Yes."

Next day I began travelling in a horse-drawn buggy like the Amish. I only saw one-third of the people I could have seen with my Ford; but now I was welcome in every yard. These people did not believe in my books, but they could tell I was doing this, travelling in this rig with horse, to please them, and it flattered them, and they showed their appreciation by buying my books—from thirty-five to sixty a day; and they fed me with lunch and supper to boot! It is this sort of thing I mean: we as Christians must do, or give up, or display, in order to win. Things in the flesh mean so much. Often, it is through these idiosyncrasies of the flesh that we lead people into the Spirit.

CRUCIAL MOMENT IN SOUL-WINNING

Always remember these MUSTS. First, build up your topic on faith. Make it a solid premise of your ministration to the person whose soul you are preparing to be saved by Christ. Once he is familiarized with who and what our Lord Jesus is, and how faith can accomplish all the things he cannot do for himself, then draw out the knowledge of sin. Get him to look at sin abstractedly, in the third person. Show him, "All have sinned, and come short of the glory of God" (Rom. 3: 23). Point out, "The wages of sin is death, but the gift of God is eternal life through Jesus Christ our Lord" (Rom. 6: 23).

Stagnate sin as sin, fear and death. Do it in the same manner as Nathan once did, by conjuring up a descriptive picture which from your former conversation is tailored to fit your subject's experience. Bring the sin, by your power of description, like a flood on his conscience. David caught on, and his conscience reacted. Then, when you have shown sin, his sins by depiction, you will be able to discern whether you have touched his conscience. If you haven't, move in tighter by quoting John 3: 16, showing how God loves him. As you note him applying your picture of sin, then your confident inclusion of him in God's love, lead him on to a "godly sorrow and to repentance", by coming back clearly to the need for faith in our Lord Jesus Christ who suffered for him, died for him, arose for him on the third day, and thus opened for him the vista of eternal life. Spell it all out succinctly as having been done for him. Quickly affirm a firm hope for forgiveness, the moment repentance comes, and lead him on to an act of faith. Quote John 5: 24, "Verily, verily, I say unto you, he that heareth my word, and believeth on him that sent me, hath everlasting life, and shall not come into condemnation; but is passed from death to life."

Led this way, your subject will have come to the stage of despair in himself, and from your firm and radiant testimony of experience and Scripture will he be elicited to place all of his hope in Jesus Christ. As he does that, immediately excite him to believe that the righteousness of Jesus Christ is now his own. If you succeed here, you will have helped him to become fully unburdened, and the phenomenon of an actual transfer of his many heavy sins upon our Lord Jesus Christ is accomplished. *This is the secret of soul-winning.* You will subsequently, indubitably, lead such a heart to salvation in the inner man (1 Cor. 15: 55–57).

CHAPTER VI

HOW TO ORGANIZE THE TRAINING, TEACHING AND TELLING PLAN

(Acts 2: 41–47)

STATING THE PROBLEM

ENTERING now upon that phase of our discussion where we approach the kernel of Christianity's problem, we recapitulate. From what has gone on before in our depicting of Christianity as a life, *a new life*, we find ourselves looking upon twentieth-century Christianity with new eyes.

Almost to a tee, we find her condition described in Ezekiel 37—a valley full of dead bones. Here and there, her erstwhile fervor still shows, and that holds forth promise. But in the main Christianity in her most important segment no longer believes in the proper measure (Eph. 4: 7) for the Christian, which is to be a witness for Christ (Acts 1: 8). The vast mass of her so-called laymen are drowsily asleep. We cry out: Christians, Awake! In the words of Isaiah 60: 1, "Arise, shine; for thy light is come, and the glory of the Lord is risen upon thee."

In order to awaken the giant, the sleeping giant, let us take a look at what we see in Christianity.

In the cults, which are a pseudo-Christianity, we observe a strange sort of activity. In action, they represent an almost 100 per cent participation in the propagation drives across the board. Since they advocate a proselytizing outreach, using horizontal drawing power, as exemplified most clearly by the Jehovah's Witnesses, they interest us because in method they have borrowed the NEW TESTAMENT WAY OF PREACHING. They challenge us because of this practice, for they have achieved total participation in this outreach enlisting fully every single adherent. THEIR PEOPLE ARE AWAKE.

Looking into present-day historic Christianity, we see a

complete absence of the use of the NEW TESTAMENT WAY OF PREACHING. Assembled in fellowships in varigated churches and associations, Christianity exists on a social tableau predicated upon the "doctrines once delivered to the saints" on one hand, and a peculiar conformity of behaviour on the other hand. The big question is not, do we in historic Christianity have the right doctrines, for that is fully resolved for us in Holy Writ, generated as these are and upheld by the Holy Spirit (Eph. 2: 20–22; 4: 4–6). The big question is, do our churches and associations create a spiritual place and atmosphere wherein a born-again life can breathe and grow from childhood to become a man in Christ, developing every one to fill his measure in Christ (Eph. 4: 7) by fitting each out to go outside of the camp to show forth the praises of God?

COMPARISON

I have always said that there is no profit in comparing the doctrines of heresies with the doctrines once delivered to the saints. The first are the product of reasoning, causing a creature to look upon God in the vesture of wrath (Rom. 1: 18–26). The latter are the result of revelation from on high, bringing in an evangelical knowledge by looking upon God in trust in the vesture of love (John 1: 14–18).

On this basis we cannot determine the true doctrines, for such comparison is but academical.

In our discussion in the past four chapters, however, we have touched on the true touchstone for comparison. We have observed that Christianity is neither a religion nor a philosophy (Col. 2: 8). It came crystal-clear to us that Christianity *is a life, a new life*, of one born-again person, and an entering into the circle of Jesus Christ. We observed that when a soul is saved, and in faith finds the righteousness of God which comes into the heart of the saved one, then such an one must begin to breathe in witnessing, and grow in grace and truth. Such growth could only come by, and through, the Holy Spirit and the Word of God. It is here, where we began to understand that churches and associations of historic Christianity are functionary precincts primarily (not social gatherings), wherein such new-born babes in Christ are weaned, fed milk, taught how to acquire a taste of strong meat, and where they must reach maturity. Important in this growth process for this new

life is the training to become a witness for Christ, an evangelizer and soul-winner, which is the measure for every
Christian (Eph. 4: 7; 2 Cor. 10: 13). It is by the praises of
the lips, we found, that such a new Christian or new creation
breathes, producing even a metabolic fragrance of the new
life, making it distinctly unique of the individuality (identity)
as that of the flower (Matt. 6: 28; Luke 12: 27), or as distinctly different in twinkle as is star from star (1 Cor. 15: 41),
as Paul puts it in describing the true individuality of life in
Christianity.

Then, in the first chapter, and again and again in allusions,
we have seen the J.W. heresy in action. Here we have seen a
total absence of the true foundation of the new life, namely,
"Jesus Christ, the same yesterday, and today, and forever."
A denial of the deity of Christ has made it impossible for the
Lord to come into the heart of a J.W., and thus the pre-
requisite of entering into the new life circle is absent. Because
of this lack the NEW WORLD SOCIETY of Jehovah's Witnesses
cannot enter into the new circle of life in Jesus Christ. They
had to conjure up, in its stead, a new society based upon flesh
and the Adamic relationship. Because this is so is why they
were able to generate a proselytizing drive which encompassed
all into a herd-like mentality, resulting into a tremendous mass-
action. Their indoctrination, their training, their organization,
all tend to bring in a sameness and an alikeness or a get-
togetherness, which eradicates the "likeness and the image
of God", namely, the individuality of each adherent, *or his
identity*.

What do we have here now? If historic Christianity uses
her churches and associations as places of assemblies for training, teaching and telling (Acts 2: 41–47), she will produce
full-grown men in Christ, who exercise their senses properly,
knowing good and evil, and everyone of whom can give an
account of his faith. This would result in their becoming true
sheep of the Lord, who, like sheep, would bring increase of new
sheep into the Church.

If the NEW WORLD SOCIETY of the Jehovah's Witnesses, and
any other cult, uses her kingdom halls, meeting places for
training, teaching and telling, they would labour under a
great disability, namely, the departure from the faith, or the
basis for the universality or catholicity of the Church (Acts 2:
42). The Holy Spirit distributes diverse gifts only within the

framework of a Christianity which is based on universally revealed doctrines (1 Cor. 12 and 13. Read these chapters very carefully). Because of this departure, Jehovah's Witnesses and the cults, in their training centres, can only produce robots and a sameness of the beast-herd. These, to be sure, can give a good account of their organization-sponsored teachings, and also can induce others to be led into it. They do bring increase to their organizations, by proselytizing, which is what slaves do; but sheep move in a different milieu. For sheep are born, and slaves are made.

If we in historic Christianity are not producing in our churches and associations the right kind of atmosphere as a spiritual place, then there can be no spirit-begetting, no spiritual growth of our children in Christ, our babes in Christ. We have the doctrines, the gospel of Jesus Christ, the Word of God, the pastors, teachers and evangelists, which make for the universality or catholicity of the Church; but we bring forth most definitely a failure in identity of each individual in performing the measure of the Spirit and the gift (1 Cor. 12; Eph. 4: 7; Acts 2: 41–47; 2 Cor. 10: 13) as an expert witness, to whom alone has been given the place as a sheep who in the process of increase *via* new birth alone can bring forth other sheep. Few pastors, teachers and evangelists bring forth sheep. Their very education and training produce a behaviour which is conserving, stabilizing, methodizing, etc. We most definitely have today an IMBALANCE IN HISTORIC CHRISTIANITY. We have the universality of the Church, but we lack the identity of the individual in reaching the "fullness of the stature of a man in Christ" (Eph. 4: 13). How have we lost sight of this? How did this come about?

PANORAMIC VIEW

For a brief background sketch which is made necessary in order to graphically depict the reasons for the losing sight for the need for the NEW TESTAMENT WAY OF PREACHING, I want to list a few facts. In stating our problems, in the previous paragraphs, we noted the absence of personal evangelism and witnessing in our midst. How did this departure from proper practice come about?

Beginning with Augustine, there came a gradual attempt to fruition to couch Christianity into the garb of a philosophy.

Subsequently a group of men who became widely known as "Schoolmen", developed a philosophy which we can term "Other-worldliness". Its purpose was to put the emphasis on the life hereafter, in heaven or hell. It played down altogether the life in the flesh, as being unimportant. All that was demanded of a life in the flesh was that it conform to the laws and the customs of the Church, making the Church responsible for the end-effect of such a life. In other words, they spiritualized living on earth to such a degree that they sacrificed the common sense of the flesh.

In our life in the flesh, it is a known fact that the entire human race have in common the same type of body, a body of flesh. In this sense, in the similitude of our body of flesh alone, are we all more or less alike.

"Other-worldliness", as concocted by the "Schoolmen", was a philosophical attempt, as I will show in that section of the CHRISTIANITY TRIUMPHANT series, which deals with this subject, to create the same commonness of life after the Spirit in heaven. Everything on earth, in the body, as a result of this focus, became bagatelle and superfluous. This kind of thinking brought about the loss of sight of many things about the natures of man, and is directly responsible for losing sight of the NEW TESTAMENT WAY OF PREACHING in the realm of historic Christianity today.

The reaction to the "Other-worldliness" of the *Sumna Theologica* came in the appearance of another philosophy, known as "This-worldliness", or the age of reason. This runs to another extreme, by playing down a life in the hereafter, and putting all the emphasis on our life in the flesh. It has had a devastating effect upon the thinking of millions, who have lost sight of all spirituality.

The nineteenth century saw the appearance of still another philosophy, namely, "Outer-worldliness" of the Seventh Day Adventist, the Christian Scientist, the Jehovah's Witness, and the Mormon, and cults innumerable. These created a chimera based on an age-old verity. They fastened onto the NEW TESTAMENT WAY OF PREACHING, using the ancient precepts on the natures of man and on the new man in Christ, and created a pattern of "OUTER-WORLDLINESS", or a coming Kingdom of a thousand years in the flesh, Adamic flesh, by establishing the philosophy of a life now in societies as a pre-requisite to the coming life in the kingdom of flesh.

To make this real, they created a work theory bringing in a works-righteousness. To be of the group it became mandatory to witness for and of the precepts of the organization. They have thus raised the battlecry to our problem: ORGANIZATION OR CHRIST: which?

Herein lies then the challenge of the cult to Christianity!

In historic Christianity, it becomes quite clear to us, we have to shed the effects which "Other-worldliness" and "This-worldliness" have produced in our churches and associations. This we can do only by fully cleaning the house of philosophy in our midst. Out with her, lock, stock, and barrel! We must once again fully accept that Christianity, and it alone, *is the true universal*, completely uniting once again in the two natures of man into a man in Christ, with a new beginning after the Spirit, born of water and the Spirit (John 3: 6). In time Christianity will be totally triumphant, not because it is a life in this world of flesh, or because it holds forth a life in the next world in the spirit, *but because it is the merging of both natures; heaven and earth, into a new creation, which will neither be cosmic, material, temporal, but the true universal life in Christ, eternal life in immortality* (2 Tim. 1: 10).

You have already seen how such a life begins in faith in Jesus Christ, of how it breathes by witnessing and grows in grace and truth, and of how it becomes united in Christ (Eph. 4: 12–15). How this new life breathes in witnessing and grows in grace and truth, will now be demonstrated.

A TRAINING, TEACHING AND TELLING PLAN (Acts 2: 41–47)

It would be more than foolish to look at this problem and then to forget it.

Once we fully understand that Christianity is the new life of a man in Christ, we will at once perceive the need to translate such a life into a pattern for "living". Fully cognizant of the fact that the mature Christian is united as a bride would be with her husband, with our Lord Jesus Christ, we realize that such a union can only become fruitful, that is, bring increase, if it produces an outreach. Witnessing, evangelizing and soul-winning, therefore, appear for us today to be the IMPERATIVE.

In the midst of Christianity much good work is being done. Much fruitful work. There is also a lot of labour of love performed which brings no tangible results of a spiritual nature. Why? Because in the main sight has been lost of what should be accomplished. What is our aim? What is our concept in Christianity? Of our church affiliation? Yes, of our church programme. Do we merely want to create physical alikeness in our behaviour, for the sake of insuring that we shall have a spiritual alikeness because of such conformity in the flesh? That was the blunting effect that the "OTHER-WORLDLINESS" philosophy had on the Christian Church. Or are we trying to produce independent personalities who conform only outwardly to our pattern of what is right, but inwardly decide when and how, or whether at all, we shall witness for our new way of life? That would be close to the nefarious philosophy of "This-worldliness" which produces the crass independence in flesh, a pattern which constantly agitates and divides in thinking, behaviour, and finally in revolutions, forming, first cliques, then parties; finally new sects. That is what is wrong with this age of reason. As long as it lasts, it will always be revolutionary, and no ecumaniacs at higher levels can contain it in our midst.

The time has come not only to ask the right questions, but also to get the right answers. The cults, in their effective use of the NEW TESTAMENT WAY OF PREACHING, are forcing us to get the answer. It is simply this: we must learn to use the NEW TESTAMENT WAY OF PREACHING and, in true universal fashion of Christianity, we must be trained to use it on a crash programme basis. It is to us a life-and-death problem. Every single individual must be trained to become an expert in its use. How can this be done?

Here is a plan:

A

Soul-winning core
Pastor-pulpit
Teachers
Leaders

B	C
(1) Witnessing	(1) Bible reading
(2) Slanted Bible study	(2) Family Bible study
(3) Prayer meeting	(3) Bible studies in homes of interested ones.
This meeting, held once a week, has the church as its centre, and must be slanted in group witnessing.	The home is the centre here.

Church Library

D

(1) Inductive training
(2) Teacher-pupil-witnessing
(3) Soul winning

Locale THE SUNDAY SCHOOL	Witnessing in the neighbourhood.
For advanced in age over twelve.	
(1) Use printed page	
(2) Use invitation for special events	
(3) Draw children of unchurched	
(4) Create liaison with unchurched parents	

As you read in my book *Thirty Years a Watch Tower Slave*, I lived through the entire phase of the development of the present-day world-wide NEW WORLD SOCIETY of Jehovah's

Witnesses. I also had an active part in the development of the seven-step programme along lines of methodizing.

However, since many of the above methods are coloured with heresy, that is, in practice, I was very careful to lay Scriptural groundwork for expounding the need of each individual in historic Christianity to share in this work, as this is his individual measure given him by Christ (Eph. 4: 7). As you have read the chapter on "Witnessing for Christ" (Acts 1: 8), you had illuminating proof offered you to see the need for personal witnessing. Then in the chapter "Evangelizing for Christ", much material was brought to your attention which shows the value of the personal contact. Finally, in the chapter on "How to Win Souls", I brought you face to face with the reality of life in Christ. It becomes real when a soul is won by God in full worship, as it wins other souls for Christ as an act of worship or as a fruit of God. To win a soul is a work that transcends all other work in value, in this world or in the next. A soul, as the Lord Jesus put it in Matthew 16: 26, is worth more than a whole world. Other worlds, or this world, or outer worlds, have nothing whatever in common with the true universal, which *is* Christianity. When a soul is thus drawn into this new circle of life in Jesus Christ it is drawn into reality. It lives forever, whereas worlds die.

THE PULPIT IS THE SOUL-WINNING CORE

As you look upon the plan I have spread before you, you will observe that while it gives an overall picture of the ideal church organization in action, it breaks this training and studying aspect down into four cardinal phases, marked A, B, C, and D. In the centre of it all is the church library. On the top of it all, and marked as the core of soul-winning, is the pastor-pulpit leadership, which is ably supported by teachers and church leaders. Only such persons should be teachers and leaders, elders, deacons and trustees, who are so in fact, and not uninitiated ones raised because of good looks, contributions, or favours.

As we go into explanation of this TRAINING, TEACHING AND TELLING plan, always bear in mind that we are presently challenged by the cults and isms in this field. The cults and isms have achieved an almost 100 per cent participation of all adherents in propagating the proselytizing drives. We in

Christianity have put the entire burden and operation of that sort of work, the getting of the increase, etc., upon our pastors and teachers. This group, however, only represents a minority in our congregations. The upshot of this is, that the cults and isms have been all thoroughly trained and equipped, whereas in Christianity we still endeavour to do a world-wide work of soul-winning by indulging in the luxury of only using a trained minority. With this minority we hope to draw the masses of mankind growing like mushrooms unto Christ. It is here, where the success of the cults and isms presents a challenge to us.

For four hundred years now historic Christianity of the Protestant persuasion has played down the usefulness of its most numerous adherents, the laymen. Emphasis was laid on the work of pastors, teachers and evangelists, whom we hired. Our laymen, therefore, by this background, by lack of training, are entirely incapable of being transformed into witnesses overnight. They have never lived according to New Testament precepts, as depicted for instance in Acts 2: 46, 47; 5: 42. As a matter of fact, many pastors have found it wellnigh impossible to get laymen to realize that it is their duty (Matt. 28: 19, 20) to go out preaching and witnessing for Christ (Acts 1: 8). Some of our churches are even so foolish that they call a visitation programme to get everyone to meet his pledge, witnessing. Our urgent need in Christianity is not more church buildings, building funds and money: *it is for more confessors.* We already have too many professors.

In fact, from what I have been able to see in the forty-eight different denominations I worked in I come to the conclusion that pastors and church leaders upon whose hearts the Lord puts the burden to accept the challenge of the cults and isms must settle at this stage, to be satisfied to work with a minority in their churches, the majority being totally unfit. Once you make that decision, pastor or church leader, then, and only then, undertake the establishment of a definite training, teaching and telling plan or programme. That will be a beginning. An important beginning. For thereafter you will make certain that every new convert coming into your church, and all children coming under your care, will be properly trained and equipped from the beginning of their spiritual lives in Christ to know no other way of behaviour than that of being a witness for Christ (Acts 1: 8).

A pastor, so burdened, and seconded by teachers and leaders with a similar burden, should then undertake the positions of a training, teaching ministry, which covers four main phases.

A. MESSAGES FROM THE PULPIT

Aside from messages designed for edification, there should also be, from time to time:—

(a) Messages about the rôle so-called laymen played in the early Church. Show how the first Christian martyr was a layman, namely, Stephen. Why? Because he was an active witness for Christ. Show how Luke, the beloved physician, was a layman. Don't forget Philip, whom we discussed in one of the earlier chapters. Raise up the ruined estate of the lay-man, or the Christian witness estate, or measure given to all by Christ (Eph. 4: 7), by pointing up to what it must again become within our midst and the precincts of Christianity if we are to fulfil our mission in this twentieth century.

(b) Messages about the need for training in Bible studies. Such messages from time to time should lay emphasis on our doctrines, and on the mid-week Bible study held in our church, clarifying why they should be slanted to induce practical group-witnessing parties to emanate from it.

(c) Messages about Sunday-school purposes, constantly out-lining, then emphasizing weak points, guiding all classes towards actual training. Show the need to qualify in the morning for advance groups going out witnessing in the after-noon or early evening.

(d) Messages about the art of home Bible studies, first in the home of the Christian and his family, then in the homes of contacts the Christian makes during his witnessing tours.

With a constant supervision by the pastor and elucidation of weaknesses overcome by timely sermons, much can be done to spark the entire training plan into a co-ordinated advance. In this plan, meaning the pulpit: pastor, teachers and leaders *must become the sparking-plug.* That is why they are the leaders, *they must lead,* not by ineffectually sermonizing, but by acce-lerated sermonizing. They must understand and be co-operative towards realization of the master-plan, and must lend them-selves, under the pastor's guidance always, to taking the lead.

B. STUDYING—WITNESSING—PRAYER MEETING

The usual mid-week meeting in our churches should be revolutionized. It should become a three-fold meeting. Its time should embrace from 7 to 9.30 p.m. It is a *bona fide* training session, and therefore should not be considered a one-hour worship service.

The first phase of the meeting should last one hour, and should begin at 7 p.m. sharp. A short prayer, then instructions and assignment to a car group. Each car group to cover a few nearby blocks of residential sections. Each, or in pairs, since it will be evening, should go from house to house to find people who are interested in studying the Bible. For example, approaches like this can be used: "We are going from house to house to find people who are interested in studying the Bible. Are you at present studying it?" If the householder says, "Yes", reply, "Fine. We are having a Bible study in church [mention name and location of your church] tonight at 8 p.m. Would you come and join us in it, and lend us your thinking on it?" If the householder replies "No" to your first query, say, "We are having a Bible study in our church [mention location and time and name of church] tonight at 8 p.m. Would you come and study with us?"

Such witnessing groups can stay out half an hour, then must return to church in time for the Bible study to begin promptly at 8 p.m. You will be amazed what this will do to the thinking of the brethren. They will be stimulated. Especially so if questions came up at the doors of the people which they couldn't handle. More so will they become enthused, as time wears on and invited ones begin to attend, or better—and this will happen—when people immediately respond to their invitation, change their clothes, and come along. At 8 p.m. prompt the meeting begins. Perhaps it is best to use a regular correspondence course of the LUTHERAN BIBLE INSTITUTE, 13016 Greenwood Av., Seattle 33, Washington, or the MOODY CORRESPONDENCE BIBLE COURSE, 820 N. La Salle, Chicago 10, Illinois. One of the leaders can be the study conductor. Let this be a social-type study.

Let all participate. Let the study conductor do but two things, to wit: (1) keep order; (2) sum up. No preaching— leave that to the pastor on Sunday. Just studying and discussing. A well-thought-out study course should be used.

Objections have been raised at this point, namely: if new ones are constantly allowed to join, then the study will never progress. That need not be. Since you are using a prescribed course, let new participants sit in on the current material, and have those brethren whose guests they are make back calls on these and assume the responsibility to bring them up-to-date. This latter is opportunity for the personal contact and evangelizing for the Christian.

When the clock strikes 9 p.m., end the study. Now invite all to participate in prayer. There will be so many things to pray about by each attending individual. Some will be burdened for some of the people they met in their witnessing period. Others will be burdened to overcome their lack of knowledge. Others will ask the Lord to undertake for specific persons on whom they are working. That prayer meeting will be charged with the Holy Spirit.

Such a witnessing, studying and praying, mid-week meeting will be the Christian's power-house of his church, as is the pulpit the pastor's ministry of the Word. It will be fruitful, alongside of the ministry of the Word, without traces of Nicolaitanism, as was the ministry of the seven alongside of the apostles, becoming a mature partnership of the Church in her outreach to win and train souls (Acts 6: 1–7). After this layman ministry was established, *notice, there came the big increase in the church* (Acts 6: 7). That is the way to do it.

C. THE HOME BIBLE STUDY: FAMILY AND NEW ONES

While A, the soul-winning core or the pulpit, and B, the witnessing-slanted mid-week witnessing, study and prayer meeting, dealt with the church-centred programme, we now come, in section C, to its main aim. The aim is a three-fold one

(1) Bible reading by the individual Christian on a daily basis.

(2) Family Bible study on a weekly basis.

(3) Bible studies in the homes of interested people.

The pulpit focus and the church Bible study training will evoke, by their very nature of both laying emphasis on the rôle of the individual in the church and historically played by him when the universality of the church and identity of the individual were in balance, and by the stress put upon individual participation in the mid-week witnessing-studying and prayer meeting, a persistent desire for, and a growing realization of, the need for regular systematic Bible reading in the home. Here the Church must give direction by gradually encouraging Christians to witness and evangelize their neighbours and interested ones they come across.

Constant Bible reading will overcome lack of basic Bible knowledge. This will evoke, in turn, special interest in key passages to be used for soul-winning. These should be read first. Become familiar with their context. Get a clear mental picture of what surrounds these passages you are attempting to memorize. At the same time, use it as often as possible in your gospel presentation, either at the doors or in conversation with others, or in the church study.

From your Bible reading, and because of your progressive memorizing of key passages riveted to memory by constant use, you will soon have need for studying the entire Bible in a systematic way in your home. Though "There is no place like home," which may be just a cliché to many, it still really is the best place for a systematic home Bible study. In company with your loved ones of your own flesh and blood, there are really no inhibitions, and social barriers are non-existent. Here are all the makings for a fruitful study. In a daily talk-it-out-matter-of-fact-way, in language commonly used, your family will learn to share Bible knowledge in the same way they do food. You are here in the deep places of human-behaviour patterns.

Use a good Bible Correspondence Course. As you use these, develop your own technique, personal family techniques, of getting the most information out of them. Also get the type of information clear in your mind which is fully understandable to you. If you do, and if you use the development of your spiritual personality in Christ, information you have gathered in the mid-week witnessing, studying and prayer meeting, you will soon become trained to put the study across in any other home, and you will have become a true evangelizer or communicator of Christ.

Training thus becomes fruitful, if it is sparked by your desire to be a witness for Christ. Then by using the church facilities to the hilt to forward your training, you approach the final point where success can be yours, YOU BECOME A DOER. Then, by actually witnessing, evangelizing and soul-winning, will you practise what you have learned, and then you will begin to breathe rhythmically and properly, and will grow in grace and truth. Now, your new creation will be breathing and living. Soon you will develop your peculiar talents latently embedded in you. These soon will begin to be welded by the Holy Spirit with a special spiritual overtone, and some of the special gifts of the spirit (1 Cor. 12 and 13) will come to the fore in you. Your church affiliation will be like many different wonderful flowers growing in a garden. Slowly, now the Word of God, which seemed so hard to come by at first, will become the living Word (1 Pet. 1: 23, 25). By hiding the Word of God in your heart, constantly, persistently, and by using it in witnessing, evangelizing and soul-winning, your heart become filled with it. Quite naturally your mouth will overflow with it. You will be speaking a new language— the language of the new heart. You will easily heed the admonition of James 1: 22: "But be doers of the word, not hearers only."

The great calamity in somnolent Christianity today is spiritual forgetfulness. Most church attendants come under the power of the preached Word in the church spoken from the pulpit. This presentation often agitates them. They are smitten while they hear it. On their way home, they are still affected. But upon coming home they soon forget what they heard and saw of themselves. Why? Their home and personal lives are not to them the arena of living after the Spirit in Christ. In their homes they live according to the flesh; in church they attempt living after the Spirit. The Spirit loses, because they give unto it only one hour every Sunday, whereas all the hours of the week they spend in living after the flesh.

What happens to them? The apostle described this matter better than I could, when in James 1: 23–25 he says: "For if any be a hearer of the Word, and not a doer, he is like unto a man beholding his natural face in a glass, for he beholdeth himself, and goeth his way, and straightway forgetteth what manner of man he was."

If a church-oriented training programme as described in this plan is adopted, and then faithfully carried out, soon, through A, B, C and D, the church will truly exert its divine gifts of pastors, teachers and evangelists in a spiritual way. How different this will be than is the monetary and fleshly way. Bringing into play the fleshly proclivities of each, into behaviour patterns conditioned unto practical routines, as is an individual's life, as is his home life throughout the week, the church will create for its background, not the church building and its building fund, but enlarge its telling influence all week long in every home. The church will not then be something to show up in on Sunday in order to throw a few palliatives to the idea of living after the Spirit, but it will become an "assembling of the saints", or witnesses.

Such practical enlisting, studying, training, witnessing, evangelizing and soul-winning scope of all individuals, will bring about a change as radical as that depicted by James 1: 25; "But whoso looketh into the perfect law of liberty, and continueth therein, he being not a forgetful hearer, but a doer of the *work* (our italics), this man shall be blessed in his deed."

Notice the individuality in the blessing! An individual blessing to the individualized performance of a deed lays emphasis on the type of work James here projects. This whole outlook is obviously quite paramount in his entire letter. It is not a blessing which comes to all under the spell of the preacher's word as depicted in James 1: 22, but a blessing which comes to each in his doing. Every act of witnessing, evangelizing or soul-winning, you see, by the nature of things, most assuredly results in better training for the next act or task ahead. THAT IS THE BLESSING IN HIS WORK, spoken of here. Here is the true criterion for the value of training and telling, in perfect interplay with teaching.

Aspect C, therefore, is truly the aim of A and B of the church training programme. To devise a course of action *via* listening to sermons from the pulpit; through the mid-week witnessing, studying and prayer meeting, leading to a personal and systematic studying of the Bible; to memorizing passages, for use in actual work in Bible studies in other people's homes, is the purpose of this plan. Every step along the route of training automatically brings a blessing to each individual who participates in it. Growth in grace and truth will ensue. But most important of all: pastor, teacher, church leader, if you have this burden and follow this plan, or one like it, as you succeed you will have enlarged your church from its building into the home of every member, and expanded it from a mere influence for one hour on Sunday to a total influence day and night all the week long.

D. SUNDAY-SCHOOL THE SOURCE FOR CHILD EVANGELISM

Sunday-school, in the scheme of this TRAINING, TEACHING AND TELLING plan, is an intermediary training centre situated in the church.

In scope, it has two purposes: one, to augment the home training of children of consecrated parents into amalgamating their thinking with that of the church, or to bring identity into balance with the universality of the Church early in their lives; and, two, the bringing of unchurched ones in, in order to lead them to salvation.

The mind of a child has a peculiarity which we adults lose. It loves to participate in social-type studies. Stories, lessons, know-how, patterns, are easily grafted into its thinking, and become by practice vicariously, habitual to it. An idea, or an ideal, can exercise enormous influence upon the mind of a child. If a Sunday-school sets itself the task to raise up the Lord Jesus high and raised up to each and every class, each and every session, concentrating then gradually on deepening the understanding about the Lord, it will succeed in not only leading the child to Christ, but will set him firmly along the pathway of the knowledge of our Lord Jesus Christ.

Once love of Jesus becomes paramount, then love for reading and studying should be implanted. Reading in God's Word, memorizing key passages to be used to tell others, discussion periods in the higher classes, should be entirely occupied with witnessing techniques and soul-winning moves.

As adulthood approaches, the child should be trained in adult ways of living in the spiritual milieu. Pitfalls should be shown. Marriage contract should be explained. All vital matters of life after the Spirit should be contrasted to the problems which are ours in the flesh.

In other words, Sunday-school has a threefold goal: (1) Lead the child to Christ. (2) Teach him to love God's Word, training him to constantly read up on it. (3) Train him to become a living Christian, or a witness, evangelizer and soul-winner. Never let him become a dead Christian, who never witnesses.

CHILD EVANGELISM CENTRED IN SUNDAY-SCHOOL

The second purpose for the Sunday-school in a church organisation is to win unsaved children for Christ.

This type of programme should be generated from out of the Sunday-school. If the first premise of the school, raising up Jesus Christ as the centre, teaching love for reading in the Bible, and in imbuing a desire for witnessing, evangelizing and soul-winning, is properly executed, then quite naturally the school will expand into child evangelism.

The help of every child, as he grows in spiritual matters, should be enlisted. High-school clubs and Christian witnessing clubs in primary schools should be the overflow from the Sunday-school.

As children reach the age of twelve they should be encouraged, by advancing in knowledge, to make special training classes. Such special training classes should range all the way from student leadership to club leadership, to evangelizing parties.

Such children should be used to enlist, then encourage, then attend to the unchurched and unsaved children. As these are drawn in, each new child should draw the personal attention of a counsellor who would stay with the child until he is saved. Other students who have talents developed for this should be assigned to join in winning the parent for Christ.

In other words, the entire Sunday-school is the peculiar department of the church which deals progressively in child evangelism. Its end product is a mature Christian, a workman who needeth not to be ashamed of his work.

If the Sunday-school becomes the centre of child evangelism, then it will project itself beyond the Sunday-morning class period, and expand into the daily lives of all of the children involved, bringing its training into the workaday world, and will fill the minds and hearts of the young with Christ Jesus and with a study of His Word, and with the doing of good works.

The Lord will bless you, Sunday-school leaders, teachers and helpers and children, as you really put this to work. He may lead you to the ideal in youth education, by blessing you with the vision and the wherewithal to establish a Christian Day School, getting away from the pernicious influences of the world.

LESSON SEVEN

How to be Fruitful in Winning Souls for Christ

"Believe me that I am in the Father, and the Father in me: or else, believe me for the very works' sake" (John 14: 11) declares the principle of faith in the doctrine of God, which underlies all successful soul-winning.

Jesus declared that He performed works intended to make them believe that the Father was in Him and that He was in the Father. His works therefore, performed in His body, were done to win souls.

Unlike our Lord Jesus, who had a perfect body without sin, we Christians are cleansed in faith by the works of Jesus, and then are told in John 14: 12: "Truly, truly, I say to you, he who believes in me will also do the works I do, and greater works than these will he do, because I go to the Father."

PATTERN SET

The pattern set here for us by the Lord is, that our faith in Christ as God and Saviour, one with the Father, is solidified by the Lord's works in the flesh. The works of the Lord were great: suffering, dying and resurrection; the least of which were His miracles. But all were the works of God, the Father in Christ.

How could such works be topped? Yet, Jesus proclaims that His disciples would do works greater than He. In what way could that be?

The Lord's miracles, and preaching, while great, dealt only with a small corner of the earth, and lasted for but three-and-a-half years. Because the Lord had gone to the Father, as He promised He would, the Christian became enabled to do works greater than the Lord Jesus did while in the flesh.

For two thousand years the Gospel, Baptism, the Sacrament have changed the lives of millions from the flesh to the spirit. Miracles played a role, but the witnessing, preaching, converting work of Christianity has been greater in time and scope than that of our Lord Jesus while on earth. In this manner not only were the Lord's works in John 14: 12 fulfilled, but here two valuable facets in our faith are proven:

one, that Jesus is in the Father and the Father is in Him, that they are ONE, and that those of us blessed with such faith are empowered miraculously to become soul winners, which turn out to be both works and fruits.

The full force of this comes home to us as we read an ancient evaluation of soul winning: "The fruit of the righteous is a tree of life" (Prov. 11: 30). What is soul winning then, a fruit or a work?

The answer is: soul winning is the art of both works and fruits, of a Christian who has in Christ, by faith, become a good tree, and who now bears fruits. "The fruit of the righteous is a tree of life; and he that winneth souls is wise" (Prov. 11: 30).

BODY PERFORMS WORKS

If witnessing for Christ is advertising Christ as we saw elsewhere, and evangelizing for Christ is the personal contact with a lost soul, then soul winning is the wise combination of both of the above. Its proper use is an art.

The proof that it is an art lies in its success, which largely depends on faithful use of our testimony of what the Lord means to us, and to our follow-through in training lost ones to study God's word.

Because the works of our Saviour, His suffering, dying and resurrection, brought us the righteousness of God, which came to us because we believed it, we now live after the Spirit. Our body of flesh is held now in subjection by being shaped daily into subjection to Christ.

Because of our faith in Jesus Christ, and due to our having become a good tree of life, our body begins to be used to approach other lost ones, who have the same body in common with us. Charitable works, educational works, rehabilitation works, all done in the flesh, are valid only if we use them wisely—namely, not as a means to an end to prove our religiosity, but rather as an opening to press in on a lost one with love. The using of our body, and its works towards others, to become friendly with them, is a wise use of it. Why? Because it is done in accordance with the will of a Father who wants all sinners to be saved, and who will bless such works, and put power in them. In this manner we ourselves grow in strength.

THE SOULS BEAR FRUITS

Since the body of a Christian, subjected in this life to Christ, is held in successful subjection only if used for good works towards others, does this mean that it bears fruits?

It is the soul of the righteous that bears fruits. The fruits of the Spirit, as Paul shows in Galatians 5: 22, are "love, joy, peace, longsuffering, gentleness, goodness, faith".

In other words, before we became Christians, we bore the fruits of the flesh, which are "adultery, fornication, uncleanness, lasciviousness, idolatry, witchcraft, hatred, variance, emulations, wrath, strife, seditions, heresies, envyings, murders, drunkenness, revellings and such like" (Gal. 5: 19–21).

As we witness for Christ, we practise giving our testimony of Jesus and we practise bearing spiritual fruits.

This teaches us two things: (1) witnessing is every good work done in our body because of our faith in Christ; (2) evangelizing is every spiritual fruit we bring to bear upon a personal contact.

It is this faithful performance of works in the body, together with bearing spiritual fruits we bear in teaching God's Word, that results in winning souls. For the artful use of both, the testimony of Jesus and the Word of God is what brought about the winning of souls (Rev. 20: 4).

Plan, then, to witness by mouth, with your hands and hearts, in order to attract sinners to the Lord Jesus, as the Lord did works and miracles amidst the Jews to attract them to the Father. But do not stop there. When you have attracted them, as the Lord did the sinners, tax collectors, harlots and others, then make personal contacts with them, and there teach them two things: (1) the Word of God; (2) display your faith in Jesus by bearing fruits of the Spirit before them (Gal. 5: 22). This combination is an art. In this way, the Lord will bless your works, and your wisdom to win souls with them will appear in winning such sinners for Christ.

It is a simple, definite method of applying the testimony of Jesus and the Word of God. Out of this simple combination, made operative by your faith and trust in Jesus Christ, you will not only win souls but also grow yourself in the process in spiritual blessedness.

LESSON EIGHT

How a Church can Counteract the Inroads of Heresy

Opposers of the church, family and state, who use heresy as a means of propagation, usually shy away from direct attack in order to win converts. From ancient times they have used the devil's tactics, as displayed in Eden already, of infiltrating the home where men live (Gen. 3: 1). So particularly effective had this method become that Paul warningly wrote to Timothy (2 Tim. 3: 5, 6, 7), "Having a form of godliness (i.e. seemingly studying God's Word), but denying the power thereof: from such turn away. For of this sort are they which creep into houses (for book and Bible studies), and lead captive silly women laden with sins, led away to diverse lusts (an allusion to Eve's predicament), forever learning and never coming to a knowledge of the truth."

The Pharisees were past masters of this tactic of infiltrating when either husband or pastor was away, or the head of house or church. We read in Matthew 23: 14, "Woe, Pharisees, hypocrites, for ye devour widows' houses, and for a pretence make long prayers; therefore receive ye the greater damnation."

Jehovah's Witnesses work like that too. They insinuate themselves into the home, get hold of one of the members of the family, usually the weakest, and gradually, under the guise of Bible education, brainwash and take such a member of the family captive. If husband or wife are involved, once one partner is won, they will proceed through such to blackjack the other into submission, or else cause a situation which results in a divorce.

Coming upon families who either have no church affiliation or who are presently not active, Jehovah's Witnesses insinuate themselves into such homes. This, too, is done under cover. The pastor usually does not hear of this study until it is too late. Usually such families who allow such studies in their homes are either rebellious at heart or have conscience trouble, for which they blame the pastor. Thus they will not tell him of what is going on. Or, if a family have conscience trouble, they will entertain such a study. Something in the church does not satisfy them.

HOW TO DISCOVER AND DEAL WITH CAPTURING TACTICS
OF CULTS

In this chapter, containing the TRAINING, TEACHING AND TELLING PLAN, we are receiving information on what to do as far as the Church is concerned.

From the success of the under-cover tactics of Jehovah's Witnesses in the homes of people we must realize that the Church is failing to exert its week-long influence upon the homes of its people. Most churches are only able to do so on Sunday, via the sermon. In this respect the sermon is highly overrated.

Irregular attendance at church, failure to participate in church programmes, in Sunday-school, are symptoms of spiritual coldness or, better, lukewarmness. Rather than constantly visit and encourage such to come to church, move in with training. How? Have a mature member conduct a home Bible study in that home, once a week, leading such through a well-organized and disciplined course on a gospel.

How will a church get such a force of mature Christians trained who are capable of teaching in homes? For it is evident that the church programme to deal with such in church has failed and must now exert itself into the home.

Follow the suggestions made in this chapter: TRAINING, TEACHING AND TELLING PLAN. The church of which I am a member, The Faith Lutheran Church, Youngstown, Ohio, has appointed me to conduct, for twenty weeks, a Bible study on the Gospel of Mark. Both the Board and the Pastor have approved of it and have given me complete charge. We are using the Lutheran Bible Institute correspondence course on the Gospel of Mark. In its sixth meeting the study is already a huge success, some twenty-two are advancing in know-how, using this very same course in the homes of irregular members. But this also makes available trained Christians for use (1) when a family is becoming infected with J.W. study; (2) when one member of the family becomes deeply involved with J.W.s; (3) when neighbours who are unchurched are being made captive.

A trained group of Christians in the art of disciplined Bible study can thus be invaluable (1) to arouse delinquent members; (2) to win new searching souls; (3) to help one member of a family to stop others from being caught; (4) to reclaim members lost to the cults; (5) to destroy a cult book study.

(1) Arouse delinquent members. A Bible study by use of a correspondence pattern, conducted by a trained Christian, will bring the Word of God into the lives of such delinquents at least once a week, and instil growth in spiritual things. Remember, where the Word of God is studied, there also is God.

(2) Win new searching souls for Christ. People coming to visit our church, or otherwise responding to our witnessing, should not be left to themselves, but the church should extend its influence immediately into such homes. Not solely by pastor's visits, but by a weekly systematized Bible study conducted by a trained layman; this will do more than all the visits of the pastor. Once the Word of God begins to influence such a life, the church, through its trained and ordained pastor, can exert the proper influence. The spadework must be done by the sheep, the laymen, who really bring the increase.

(3) Help one member of a family to stop others from being caught. Usually members not caught are those who are not Christians. Still, these sense that something is wrong. Frantically a husband will try to stop his wife from becoming a J.W. Arguments and strife result, which make matters worse. Here, the church can step in, by sending a trained Christian to conduct a Bible study with both or the family. Keep it up, until the fire is put out. In the process you will win the one not infected to Christ, and, once this is achieved, he will win back his spouse, for then the Holy Spirit will work through him. In the meanwhile the study itself may reclaim the J.W. convert.

(4) Reclaim members lost to the cults. Often members of our church are caught. We should not let them alone. For they were just members, not Christians, and the fault was with us. The Lord will bless our efforts to get back into such homes, with a Bible study. Many people say they are Lutherans, Methodists, Episcopalians, Baptists. Maybe that is all they are. Spiritually a Lutheran, Methodist, Baptist, is good only if he is primarily a Christian.

(5) Destroy a cult study. If you get word of a home book-study being conducted in the home of a friend by J.W.s, get yourself invited. Then, since this is a question-and-answer style meeting, raise many questions, the answers of which contradict brainwashing processes. In this manner you will

slowly defeat the J.W. conducted Home Bible study, and strengthen the backbone of the others. Once the J.W. has been forced to leave the field, you enter in with a Bible study for twenty weeks.

This same method can also be used in congregational studies held in the Kingdom halls of Jehovah's Witnesses. As Jehovah's Witnesses invade the homes of your people, as well as their neighbours, in their proselytizing campaigns, do not stand meekly by. Be imaginative, carry the battle to the gate. How?

Jehovah's Witnesses are peculiarly subject to such infiltration tactics. They have no worship services. All their meetings, Watch Tower Study, Bible Study, Service meeting, are question-and-answer training meetings. A few well-trained Christians can do some splendid work in such a meeting. Here is how they can do it: (1) get hold of the material used in the particular study in the Kingdom halls you are going to concentrate on; (2) prepare questions so slanted they will force discussion of your beliefs; (3) engage other attendants in conversation in such a way that they think you are interested—of course you should be interested in the view of the individuals, as this will tell you how far advanced they are; (4) get names and addresses of such who appear to be weak and visit them; (5) as soon as you have such names and addresses, and while you are dealing with them, subscribe for a gift subscription of the *Converted Jehovah's Witness Expositor*, which will come into their homes; (6) finally, to become thoroughly effective, start a Bible study in that home.

Jehovah's Witnesses, in this manner, become a wonderful missionary field.

CHAPTER VII

HOW TO ORGANIZE GROUP WITNESSING

ON OUR WAY REJOICING

BEFORE us, in previously depicted scenes, lies the panorama of a new life in Christ. Its very appearance as a new life displays the power of God, because it becomes, without a shadow of doubt, THE WORK OF GOD.

As we thought our way through the discussions on witnessing to Jehovah's Witnesses, on witnessing for Christ, on evangelizing for Christ, on soul-winning and sharing our surplus in Christ, we saw in a panoramic view the power in the gospel of Jesus Christ appear into full view. That power is faith in Christ.

No sooner did the power of faith in Christ bring in the righteousness of God, than there came about a new birth, an entering into the life circle of Christ. Now, it was discerned, a growth process began in the new creation after the Spirit. A growth in works? No. A growth in faith to the point where the new creature began to breathe. This breathing manifested itself in witnessing, evangelizing and soul-winning. It brings about a liberation from the flesh, to a living after the Spirit. It also germinates a growth in grace and truth after the Spirit.

In pursuit of both facets of the new life in Christ we realised that a Christian must "study to show himself approved . . . to become a workman who need not be ashamed of his work" on one hand, and then must put this evangelical knowledge into use, by reaching out to win others for Christ.

In this manner there was laid before us the TRAINING, TEACHING AND TELLING PLAN (Acts 2: 41–47). Within the framework of this plan emphasis is not only laid upon training and teaching, but, more importantly, the training and the teaching in the church, as indulged in, brings forth know-how in training and teaching plus, telling the story of the gospel of Jesus Christ unto outsiders in order to prepare the ground of their hearts for the power of God to begin its work of God.

But all of this in the community of a church organisation would be only a sputtering here and there, unless it became a way of life in the total organization, featuring clear identity in the universal Church. The way I mean is the following in the footsteps of our Lord Jesus Christ. The becoming of a witness for Christ. For us humans, who have a strange social proclivity in our flesh, it is easier to walk hand in hand with a company of fellow humans than to walk alone. In unison with others, while in the flesh, we humans do our best work and advance farthest.

If the way of our Lord Jesus (John 14: 6) is the right way, and if we are born again into living after the Spirit, then we shall indubitably be on our way rejoicing. Willingly, we "present our bodies a holy, living sacrifice, which is our reasonable service" (Rom. 12: 1).

Blazoned across all the ages from Abel to John the Baptist, and now from Pentecost to this present time, comes this searching query: "WHAT MUST WE DO, TO BE DOING THE WORK OF GOD?" (John 6: 28).

Is this a valid question? Is it a sincere question? In the climax of their history a whole nation once claimed to be doing the work of God. In displaying evidences of their works, which they claimed were performed in the service of God, the Jews laid special emphasis on their use of certain foods, the performances on special days, and, above all, their adherence to the law and to Moses.

Fastening on to the miraculous manna sent from heaven to their ancestors (John 6: 31), they laid claim to having a special kind of food. So important had this eating of special foods, keeping of special days, performing of special rites become to them, that they claimed they were doing the WORK OF GOD. Feeding their flesh, giving alms, performing certain rites, had become to them the whole service of God, resulting in feeding their flesh, gaining riches and honour in it on earth.

Scanning the history of the Jews, and evaluating the pull of feeding the flesh on the thinking of those involved, we see that this intruding of food for the sake of satisfying the flesh led to false claims. If that is so, if this leads to making false claims as to what the work of God is, then we have before us a monumental query:

IS FOOD ENOUGH?

So important was food in the thinking of the Jew that he would evaluate a prophet, or a teaching, solely upon being favoured by either teacher or prophet with the outward token of feeding himself and his flesh. That had become second nature to the Jew. He looked for signs, wonders and miracles to feed his flesh, yearning for a land of milk and honey.

Today, in historic Christianity, in wide sections of it, far too much emphasis has been laid on the special brand of food concocted by the denomination, and adherents often will only listen to a preacher if he favours them with these special idiosyncrasies tantalizing their appetite. This special food, or denominational teaching, often different from the Bible or the Word of God, makes for rules for that body, marking and designating what the works for the Lord are.

But looking at John 6: 26–27, we observe the Lord Jesus telling the Jews why they were following Him. Was it because of His teachings or His miracles? No. It was because He had filled their bellies in the miracle of the bread. In raising this query at this particular moment in His ministry, the Lord wants to indicate what sort of disciples the teaching of the gospel attracts. They are not all born again.

By the hundreds of millions the people to this day come to the churches of historic Christianity, where the gospel is still being preached, to hear the proclamation of this gospel as though they were sincere disciples. It is quite common in Christianity to regard the gospel as a belly sermon: "What kind of food shall I eat; what kind of drink shall I drink?" Whole denominations base their gospel message on special days, moons, foods, drinks and dress and behaviour patterns peculiar to themselves and their association.

Man being a social animal, these are some of the proclivities of the flesh. However, to re-establish flesh, or the way of flesh, is not the reason why Christ shed His blood. The gospel of Jesus Christ is a proclamation about the glory, praise and honour of God (as we saw in the chapter on "Soul-winning, a Sharing of our Surplus in Christ"). In preaching this gospel, our pastors should not only emphasize its power and faith unto salvation, but also should excite us more to become witnesses for Christ, directing ourselves individually to the praise of God and to the glory of Him. Why? God wants us, each new-born one after the Spirit, to use our lips (Rom. 10: 10; Heb. 13: 15) to praise and laud Him and to do what pleases Him. Such is the alchemy of living, our witnessing, becoming a breathing of our new creation.

How do we discern that? When we seek first God's honour and His kingdom (Matt. 6: 33), He, in turn, offers to give us not only temporal life and its food, but eternal life as well.

It is an old story to regard the boons of the life in the flesh. God satisfied all our fleshly wants long ago, before He issued the gospel of Jesus Christ. You can read of this in Genesis 1: 28.

Therefore it was not to preach about matters pertaining to the flesh that Christ Jesus came to preach. Those Jews followed Him for a free hand-out. They had no regard for His food and His miracles.

Does it surprise us if today whole groups of so-called disciples are more concerned about their physical well-being than for Christ to feed them eternal food? Seeking to hear the gospel for self-gratification: such eventually, when persecution comes upon Christendom (which it will soon in total waves, as the world becomes atheistic and totalitarian), will frantically seek the true gospel, and will have a hard time of it.

Take for an example the Jews. Today, these Jews who once refused to hear the gospel of Jesus Christ would be glad to pay a king's ransom to have an apostle, a prophet sent to them (as of old); but they will hear them no more!

Thus here the Lord handles the Jews this way. The gospel is not intended to give food and drink, house and home, wife and children. It is intended to give us something superior to that. The gospel of Jesus Christ is not given to instil greed, or a sense of smugness, or a spirit of indolence.

At the time of man's creation God ordered him to cultivate the garden (Gen. 2: 15). Becoming disobedient, man's labour became hard, God imposing heavy toil on him, obliging him to eat bread in the sweat of his brow (Gen. 3: 19).

The Lord Jesus makes this point this way: "Do not labour for the food that perishes, but for the food that endures to eternal life, which the Son of Man will give you" (John 6: 27).

FLESH IS DISPLEASED

The moment the pastor begins to preach about witnessing for Christ, evangelizing for Christ, soul-winning for Christ, many in Christianity are displeased. The mere discussion of this subject has caused raised eyebrows. Is the author up to some J.W. tricks? Many faithful pastors have found it impossible to organize personal evangelism in their churches. In fact, one not so long ago told me, "My congregation do not want to see or hear from me from Sunday evening to the next Sunday morning."

How many of us spend about one-and-a-half hours on Sunday in the house of God, and the balance of the week we employ *in toto* in the pursuit of money, goods, food and drink?

In the above passage, John 6: 27, Christ places two types of food side by side: the perishable and the eternal. If you really are born again and in Christ, you would by your course of action show a distinct contempt for that which is perishable. You would not "write your name in the sand" (Jer. 17: 13), as are all perishable things, but you would daily take in—in Bible reading, key-text memorizing, and home Bible studies— the imperishable food and life, by studying and witnesses.

If you claim to be a Christian, and are only giving unto the Lord one-and-a-half hours every Sunday morning for living after the Spirit, would not that be madness and folly on your part?

CHRIST IS OUR FOOD AND SERVICE

Too long had the Jews sought the things of the earth, and called this pursuit SERVICE OF GOD. Christ directs their attention to a different supply of food, by such statements— "which the Son of Man will give you." "Why?" He continues. "For on Him has God the Father set His seal."

This kind of food cannot be acquired by works; nor can it be intelligently grasped by knowledge. The words of Christ require faith; they contain a message intended only for Christians. Only a Christian who reads, memorizes, studies God's Word, and into whose heart the Lord Jesus has come recognizes Christ by faith (John 5: 39). To such an one Christ *is* the One on whom the Father has set his seal, *to certify that He provides the food.* Only those in Christ, therefore, who feed on Christ, obtain everlasting life.

How futile were thirty years of my life as a Jehovah's Witness. I had become totally addicted to the Watch Tower magazine as "providing food in due season", and as long as I fed on it I was on my way to perish.

How proud many of us in Christianity are of our brand of

religion. Our pet doctrines. Our great works. Our beautiful church buildings, colleges, hospitals; our influence as an organization wielding influence in the world.

How clever are the doctrines of pagan religions of the world? How artistic their temples, images, and icons? Their ancient rites are impressive.

How reasonable are the statements of modern science? What are all of these enumerated specialities of the human mind and genius for organization, and the forging of institutions? All are so many different brands of food offered to dying mankind. Still, they are all perishable food. Why? Because they cause you "to write your name in the sand" (Jer. 17: 13).

But here note: in Christ is eternal, imperishable food, upon whom has been set the brand of eternity, the seal of the Father!

God is not a common one, He is the Father! Here he plainly says that He has but one seal, and this He has set upon Christ, His Son. He Himself spoke from heaven about this (Matt. 17: 5). He wishes to have this important fact proclaimed publicly (1 John 1: 1). Peter and the other apostles understood and believed this by saying, "You have the words of eternal life" (John 6: 68).

MUST WE ADD OUR WORKS TO THIS SEAL?

Those who prate about their works for God like to quote Daniel 4: 27. The effect of such works of mercy and charity does not bring everlasting life—nowhere does it say that in Daniel 4? Such works have only a limited effect, and are depicted by the Lord in such passages as "make friends for yourself by means of unrighteous Mammon" (Luke 16: 9), or, "Give, and it shall be given unto you; forgive, and ye shall be forgiven" (Luke 6: 37, 38).

We can go even further than that by saying that whoever claims to be a Christian must demonstrate this with good works, charities, benevolences. Because, once the righteousness of God has come into his heart and he is born again he is a good tree, and consequently must bear good fruits (Matt. 7: 20). Good works can be done also because of tenderness and compassion often found in the flesh, and are not always a fruit of the Spirit. Frequently charities and benevolences are performed as an end in themselves, as the work of God, or work for God.

Charities, benevolences, mercy, alms, are only the first step of a good work. Since we have a body of flesh in common, the Lord wants us Christians to be charitable, in order to make friends among the lost. Once, by our kindness, helpfulness, practical assistance to the lost, we have made him think friendly of us, we must follow through here by witnessing, evangelizing and soul-winning. Otherwise we are just misusing our goods.

The Lord Jesus says, "I will give you an everlasting food, which is my flesh and blood." It is to this that the Father has set His seal. In this word God the Father forever denies to any and all teachers in the world, as well as in Christianity, any honour or merit who claim to hold solely in their organization the power to nourish me eternally. Here, the Father admonishes us, if you want eternal life, *cling to Jesus Christ*.

As you read in my book *Thirty Years a Watch Tower Slave* you will observe how the Watch Tower Society finally set itself up as the sole dispenser of "food in due season", and then arrived at the teaching that only Jehovah's Witnesses, who are obedient to the Theocracy, shall be saved in Armageddon and live thereafter on earth forever.

The food served by the Watch Tower Society is peculiar. They claim that it results from flashes coming from the temple of Jehovah, now situated somewhere in the clouds, where Christ presently resides since 1918. Having returned invisible to human eyes in 1914, He set up His temple in 1918. They claim that these flashes of light are reflected by angels of different ranks upon the minds of the *Watch Tower* editors, who in turn publish it in the columns of the *Watch Tower* magazine. This constantly changing light brings forth peculiarly tasting doctrines, resulting in outlandish behaviour patterns, all of which are designed to create a separateness of the Jehovah's Witnesses in the NEW WORLD SOCIETY from the rest of mankind. These light flashes are almost always minutely and authoritatively backed by Holy Writ. That is, apparently so. Appearing in the columns of the *Watch Tower*, they are billed as the latest of God's mind. This entire set-up will be thoroughly exposed in my coming large book *Is the New World Society of Jehovah's Witnesses Christian?*

I hope that what will therein be disclosed, embracing

organization, management, knowledge techniques, propaganda prongs, separation tactics, generating mass-action, infiltrating of Christian thinking, subverting of worldly thinking, creating issues, establishing living patterns, will become an object lesson to all Christians.

WHAT IS GOD'S WORK?

Our Lord ends the surmising by saying, "This is the work of God, that you believe on Him whom He has sent" (John 6: 29). God's work not only is what God Himself does. The term includes all divine service. A church becomes the house of God, although man built it. The psalms and prophets speak of the "works of God" in things we perform at the command of God. David was told he was fighting the "battle of the Lord" (1 Sam. 25: 28). Ezra speaks of "those who have oversight of the work of the house of the Lord" (Ezra 3: 8).

Our flesh and blood only serve themselves. They are not given to serve God or do His work. If a single work of God is to be performed by us it has to be inspired by God in the Spirit. With this in mind, the Lord's remarks take on a new meaning. The works Christ refers to are works of grace which we perform by His Spirit, which He commands, and which God requires of us. Note, such works have nothing at all to do with eating, drinking, living after the flesh, gaining mammon, keeping days, moons, performing rites, believing peculiar doctrines. *They are works Christ has commanded*, of which He speaks here. What are His commands? Matthew 28: 19, 20; Acts 1: 8; Proverbs 11: 30; 27: 17, and many others.

I suppose, in writing this training material series on WITNESSING, EVANGELIZING AND SOUL-WINNING, I am laying myself wide open to this criticism: "Who are you to teach us how to serve God? Do we not have services in our church? Do we not do charitable works? Are we not members in good standing? Do we not live a clean Christian life? Do we not support missionaries, colleges, institutions for the aged, the crippled; and hospitals?"

Christ calls all of these works food that does not keep. One that will not aid you in dying to attain eternal life. Why? Simply look at this: many worldly organizations and persons do these, and often are more generous than are you who claim this is the work of God. Like unto them, so to you, all of this is like a day that passes away and a garment that wears out (Ps. 102: 26).

Because all of this is perishable, we are admonished in Psalm 2: 12 to pay homage to Christ: "Kiss Him," and serve Him by believing on Him, and by spreading His faith to others. Everywhere in the Scriptures you will find agreement that *this* is the service of God. It is Christ-centred. The only work we have to perform, and which has any eternal validity whatever, *is to believe in Jesus Christ*. Faith, then, is the work man must do. Yet this work is also called God's work. What is the real service and work of God? It is the doctrine of faith in Christ.

Faith does not originate with us in flesh and blood. Jesus says so. "No man can come to me except the Father ... draw Him" (John 6: 44). Again He says, No one can believe in me unless it is granted him by the Father (John 6: 65). While this *is* the kind of work God demands of us, at the same time He Himself must implant it in us, for we cannot believe by ourselves.

With seven-mile boots now, we come to the crux of this discussion. If the work of God is to believe in Christ, then such faith brings in the new birth. This new life in Christ, thus generated by faith, begins to grow in faith by breathing out, or witnessing for Christ, this new life. The true work of God in us, then, is to be used by God as examples in salvation, as Jesus became in salvation our example, in order to lead others to Christ. The work of God, then, is to believe and obey Christ, becoming not only hearers but doers of the Word of God: "every man being blessed in his work" (Jas. 1: 25).

BEING TRANSFORMED INTO THE IMAGE OF CHRIST

It is after our bodies are presented "a holy, living sacrifice, which is our reasonable service" (Rom. 12: 2) that we begin to be transformed into the new mind, heart, soul, life, doing the will of God.

One of the great tasks of a Christian who is mature, and of pastors, teachers and evangelists, is to help the newly born-again Christians to overcome their breathing difficulty with which their new life begins. Stage-fright is one of the symptoms. Openly to talk about salvation and our stand on it is incongruous to the flesh; yet it must be started (Rom. 10: 10).

Be mindful that such novices are only used to talk after the flesh. Now they must be taught a new language, which is the language of the Spirit. The undertone of the language of the Spirit is a confession of Christ as our living Saviour.

Even in the world, amidst the flesh, many people have inhibitions. Some are extroverts. Others are introverts. Speaking comes hard to some. Others are shy to express themselves. Add to that the language of the Spirit, and you have a formidable task.

Bringing in 10,000's of new converts made drastic action necessary on the part of Zone servants and other leaders dealing with the training in the Theocracy. Being Zone servant in north-eastern Ohio and north-western Pennsylvania, I trained several thousands of Kingdom Publishers. Many newcomers were difficult. They would not go out from house to house, much less talk it. I devised this method to *get* them out. The last day of the month I would go through the Publishers' record file, ferret out those who had no daily report slips on file for that month, and go and visit these. I would say, "Brother, did you forget to file a report this month?" If the reply was, "I did not go out," I would rejoin, "Let us go out now for one hour. We cannot have a Kingdom Publisher spend a whole month without doing something. Get your hat and coat." Having said that, I would wait until the Publisher would come. Then I would take him out for exactly one hour, stop, return to his home, have him make out his daily report, and say, "Try to put in at least one hour before next month comes to a close." That usually worked. From my own experience, in the Theocracy, I knew that strict training at the outset would help the Publisher eventually to overcome his recalcitrance. If that is true in a system like that of Jehovah's Witnesses run by the Watch Tower exactors, who are but men, how much better results could we achieve in historic Christianity wherein the Holy Spirit regenerates and upholds?

I will give you now, by way of demonstration, a few experiences I had, as a budding Kingdom Publisher, when a lad of sixteen, just setting out, and how, being forced to witness, I matured.

When I was a lad I was very shy. Being in the presence of three or four people would lock my mouth tighter than a zipper could have. Imagine my consternation when I was told in March 1921 that I would have to go out from house to house and sell these books the Watch Tower was putting out. I thought I would die. Still, a man to whom I had been given as companion in this enterprise, insisted that I break the ice. The Company servant working through him, exerted his influence. If I did not come out on the Saturday afternoon I was supposed to meet him; he would come over and pick me up. Firm supervision took hold. Under his tutelage I gradually found some boldness. However, his tutelage did not bring true liberty, until . . . a Sunday in May, 1924, I worked an exclusive section of Berlin, in Wansee to be exact, where all of Germany's rulers of the Weimar Republic lived, he on one side of the street, I on the other.

Coming on this Sunday morning upon a pretentious villa, walking through the gate into the spacious front yard, and before reaching the entrance, I was hailed by a man who was seated in a veranda draped with beautiful lilacs to the left side of the entrance, which was shielded by shrubbery. Coming to him, my heart was in my mouth as I recognized a well-known face in German jurisprudence, a *justizrat*, as he was titled. I began haltingly to tell this jurist what I was there for. He listened, never interrupted, like a true jurist—getting my case, I suppose; and then, when I had finished, began to pick my presentation apart. I stood my ground and gave a full account of my premise. How grateful I was at that moment for all the reading I had done in Watch Tower literature, and for the pressure put on me by the organization to keep using that information in witnessing. This, by the way, was the first time I had been challenged in this manner to do so. He liked my defence, bought all eight different books I had, and gave me fifty Reichsmarks, telling me to keep the change for our work. The change was forty-one Reichsmarks.

I am not relating this experience at my being inducted into Watch Tower service in order to glorify it. I want to make a point right here. Pastors and church leaders, whenever new ones are trained to become witnesses—and that should be from the moment they are born again—never fail to be strict in raising them up. Firmness here, checking, watching, leading; in witnessing, and in reading, memorizing and studying, and DOING IT ALL THE TIME, will eventually lead your pupil in the Lord to that opportunity, when he or she will face up to the challenge, where they will be forced "to give an account of the faith that is in them".

I walked away from that experience a new man. Never thereafter was I afraid to stand up for the Watch Tower religion. I had actually defended before my betters in the world, successfully, what I believed. Here is the principle in witnessing involved—remember that which James 1 : 25 enunciated: "Every man shall be blessed in his work," meaning, it leads you on to better training. While this is true basically in all endeavours in the flesh, it is doubly true in the Spirit. In the flesh, it led me on in advances in the Watch Tower movement to unheard-of heights for a shy boy. Just look what this principle has done for me once I began to walk in the Spirit, after I came unto Christ in the spring of 1952. It led me to write two books, one of which is now published in six languages; to write several highly successful pamphlets or booklets, which are out in eighty-four languages respectively; it led me before 665,000 persons in some forty-eight different denominations; it led me to edit and publish the *Converted Jehovah's Witness Expositor*, which today goes into 108 lands, has already caused thousands to come unto Christ. In the Spirit, after which all our new-born babes in Christ will be led in historic Christianity, we can well use the above principles, because we have the Holy Spirit to generate and uphold. Leaders in Christianity, be very firm in keeping your new ones to what may appear to them the grindstone of witnessing. While they are young in this new life, while they are new, like babes, they are pliable. Don't let them acquire the bad habits of our bulk of present church members, who never witnessed and think coming on Sundays to church for an hour, to fulfil a pledge, is all that they need to grow to maturity in this new life in Christ.

Coming back now to my chain of experiences. In the autumn of that year (1924) I was called to Watch Tower headquarters in Magdeburg, Germany, to help out and be trained in the ministry. But after that, in June 1926, we were putting out all over the world a paper called *Anklage* or *Indictment*. All the rulers were to get a copy, handed to them personally together with a testimony. The Company servant of Berlin asked me to do the job, to see the President of the Weimar Republic of Germany, General Paul von Hindenburg-Beneckendorf. I prepared myself, mentally and physically; donned in my best suit, I planted myself on a Monday morning in the ante-chamber of the President's office. Mr. Mueller, the President's secretary, held out little hope. For three days I would appear in the morning at 9 a.m. and wait until 5 p.m., when the office closed. On the third day, Mr. Mueller told me that he had told his excellency about me, and that I could now see him. Here I was, a lad of twenty-one, once very shy and afraid, standing before Germany's greatest Field-Marshal, un-afraid, respectfully giving my testimony. He too queried me closely. I stood my test. He smiled, patted me on the head, and took the paper *Anklage*. That was a far cry already from my first timidity.

Then in the early days of 1927 a truck-load of us, coming from Magdeburg, were assigned to work a small town in north-western Brandenburg. I was in charge. We had finished the little town and were about to leave when a large troup of Brown-shirted men came marching towards us, equipped with heavy sticks. I knew they were going to beat us up. I told all the boys, calmly assuming responsibility: "Brethren, let us brace ourselves, fight hard if we must, and don't quiver if you go down. Maybe the Lord wants us to become the first martyrs in Germany against the Nazis." That truly perked the boys up.

But before the fight could start I decided to use persuasion. I addressed the Brown-shirts simply: "Germans, you National Socialists pride yourselves in the solidarity and purity of all true Germans. You even go so far as to say, *Am deutschen Wesen soll die Welt genesen* (In the German nature the world will become well). You are German, pure German, you aver. Here are twenty-eight of us, who too are German, pure German. I can trace my ancestry on my mother's side back to the twelfth century when already they were freemen in Southern Wuertemberg, and on my father's side in Hessia to the fourteenth century when they served the Landgraves. They were always Germans. The same holds true of my companions. How will it look before the world, who are not German, if Germans are fallen upon by Germans because of their religion, and in fight, out-numbered three to one, are beaten down because of their religion? What will the world think of your slogan about the German blood?" I noticed, as I progressed, that these men slowly shifted their feet; then one after another turned and left, until we were alone.

Persuasion had won, and that by one who at one time was even scared of his own shadow. In practice, of talking, of working, of meeting people, is where you grow. If that is true in a fleshly organization like the Watch Tower movement who deny the Holy Spirit as a person, how true it can become when used in the realm of Spirit, where the Holy Spirit is active.

To this day, when a person becomes a Jehovah's Witness, even though he knows very little as yet, he is made to go out from house to house. In a morning's tour such a one, in company with another, may say his little piece to some thirty people. These people all hear his message only once. But he, he tells this same story to himself, thirty times over, and in this manner converts himself. The above experiences show you that I gradually became stabilized in my Watch Tower thinking because of this witnessing.

As you set out to create a proper climate in your church, and begin putting into effect the TRAINING, TEACHING AND TELLING plan (Acts 2: 41–47), you will create a trend in your church. Christians, as soon as the Lord comes into their hearts, should be led to confess this great event by giving their testimony. The oftener they give it, the sooner they will become stabilized in living after the Spirit.

FORM A CONCERTED MOVE IN YOUR CHURCH

In relating these personal experiences, I am marshalling, even from the point of view of the flesh, a formidable array of facts, which lead to the evolvement of steps leading to maturity. In Christian circles this is today entirely disregarded. However, if you followed the discussion in this book you will have noted that these steps elucidate the way of our Lord Jesus: repentance, believing in our Lord Jesus as our Saviour, His righteousness becoming ours as we are born again, entering into the life-circle of Christ after the Spirit. The interplay of witnessing and believing; reading, studying and memorizing and evangelism; works of charity leading to soul-winning; accelerate a continued flow of rhythmic breathing, growth, and fitting into the measure of Christ given by Him to every new-born babe in Christ (Eph. 4: 7). This is the way of life. *On this way we should be rejoicing.* It is the way of the pilgrim in an alien land, whose city is in heaven and not in a NEW WORLD SOCIETY on this earth.

OPERATION: WITNESSING!

During the autumn months of the year select six consecutive weeks for operation: WITNESSING. Pick an evening for this move. Enlist all who come. Then, regularly, once a week for two hours, go into definite territories and witness from house to house. Different techniques, approaches and reasons can be used. These you can develop according to your task. The main object of these witnessing parties is to acquaint the people you meet, with our Lord Jesus Christ, encouraging all such to come to your church mid-week meetings for training and schooling.

At the end of the six-week period have the pastor call all of those participating, those who participated all six times, and who succeeded in bringing six new people to the mid-week meeting as a result of their work, to the front of the church on that Sunday morning. There he can lay hands on these, praising them for faithful performance, and declare, for all the church to hear, that these have proven themselves to be WITNESSES FOR CHRIST. Give them some token of the occasion.

It does not pay to have such a group effort last longer than six weeks, as longer periods will tend to slow it down. If someone starts out, and for one reason or another fails to attend the second time, go to him the next day and discuss his problem, going into prayer with him there about it to the Lord, asking the Lord to strengthen him. That usually helps.

Pastors, do not be discouraged if only a small number of your church participate. Most of them are too far gone to change overnight. They have not been breathing—that is, witnessing—since the day they were still-born, and it will take quite a slapping to quicken them spiritually to begin living after the Spirit. The nice thing about all this is, though still-born, such is the nature of this new life in Christ that these can explode any moment into breathing habits. That is what you are trying to achieve with your group witnessing operation: WITNESSING.

OPERATION: PERSONAL CONTACT

In the months of January to March set the second operation in motion for a six-week period. Call this period operation: PERSONAL CONTACT.

Once a week, for six weeks, visit people who have shown interest in your former campaign, or new ones whom you have contacted, and encourage them to have a Bible study course, such as the LUTHERAN BIBLE INSTITUTE Correspondence or Moody Bible Correspondence course.

At the end of the six-week period have the pastor call all to the front of the church on a Sunday morning who have participated throughout the six weeks, and who succeeded in starting three Bible studies. These he should declare to be Evangelizers, and so lay hands on them, approving their course of action before the assembled church, and commending their course of action to the entire church. Give them some sort of commemorative token.

OPERATION: SOUL-WINNING

The third period of six weeks should be somewhere from April to June of the year. Here, once a week, all participating should select human contacts who are in hospitals, who are in physical or spiritual needs. Sick, drunkard, hospitalized ones, jailed ones, all suffering in one way or another. In these contacts, once a week, have all participating use their common humanity as contact point. Observe, not their church affiliation; not their religion; not their doctrines—just their need. Do go unto such. Help them. But do not stop there. Learn to use benevolences as a starter, and then proceed to befriend them and bring the Lord Jesus to them. Use their afflictions as a means to bring Christ to them. The techniques described for you in my chapter, "Soul-winning, or Sharing our Surplus in Christ", should be used here.

At the end of this six-week period have the pastor call all those who participated all six times in this operation, and who succeeded in winning one soul, come to the front of the church. Have him lay his hands on them, and commend them before the whole congregation as such who are soul-winners. Give them some definite token.

In withholding commendation to all such, publicly, who either failed to participate all six times during an Operation, or who failed to get the results expected, you are creating an incentive, which will lift eventually spiritual achievement to a high level, causing many to emulate opportunities and know-how and seriousness and sincerity, all tending to win souls for

Christ. There will not only be the perfunctory doing of something, which unfortunately characterizes so much of our layman's activity in Christianity today, but big purposefulness based on results.

While only a few may participate at the outset, still it is a beginning; and soon many mature Christians in your church will be on their way rejoicing. It will be catching, and, as the second year rolls around, more will participate because the witnesses, evangelizers and soul-winners of the first year will lend an experienced hand to lead and encourage the new trainees coming after them.

The important thing is, you have established a trend. Dovetail this group witnessing plan with the TRAINING, TEACHING AND TELLING plan, which in one way or another, you must first inaugurate in your church, and you will have a constant maturing of new participants, all, being on their way rejoicing in the Lord.

As we started out, so we end; it is high time, Christian: awake!